Holocaust Poetry

COMPILED AND INTRODUCED BY HILDA SCHIFF

ST. MARTIN'S GRIFFIN
NEW YORK

ISBN 0-312-14357-5

First published in Great Britain by Fount, an imprint of HarperCollins*Publishers*

10   9

O earth, cover not thou my blood,
and let my cry have no resting place.

JOB 16:18

Contents

Destruction

(i)

(ii)

Rescuers, Bystanders, Perpetrators

Afterwards

Second Generation

Lessons

God

(i)

(ii)

INTRODUCTION

The Holocaust was a unique epoch in the experience of mankind. We use the term Holocaust, or *Shoah*, because we are at a loss as to what other words to apply to it. Chronologically it extends throughout the period of time when Hitler's ideology and regime developed and held sway over Europe in the 1930s and 40s. The Holocaust encompasses the experiences of countless surviving individuals, both Jews and non-Jews, whose lives were radically changed by it at the time and who subsequently remained affected by the repercussions of that time, even to the second generation. In a general sense however the word Holocaust is most widely recognized as signifying the death of millions of human beings who were destroyed in unimaginably cruel ways by the Nazis and their collaborators. This book bears witness to the fate of all of these.

Historical accounts of the Holocaust are now legion. Major works of scholarship are based not only on the eyewitness accounts of victims and bystanders, but primarily on authenticated documents drawn from the archives of the perpetrators themselves. Immense volumes of German state documents were recovered in 1945, and these are supplemented by more recent finds in the archives of the KGB, together with all the incriminating black and white film footage taken by the Nazis themselves, said to have consisted of six railway wagonloads at one time, until some of it was conveniently incinerated. It would therefore be invidious of me to seek to rehearse again the details of what happened. Moreover it is more than likely that the person who picks up this collection of poems will already have an outline knowledge of the subject in any case.

While the contents of this book in no sense mirror an historical survey of what occurred during the Holocaust, they are nevertheless a fundamental aid to historical understanding. The more or less contemporaneous literature of any period of history is not only an integral part of that period, but it also allows us to understand historical events and experiences better than the bare facts alone can do because they enable us to absorb them inwardly. In involving ourselves in the authentic literature of the Holocaust, we come as close as we can to entering psychologically into those unique events as they were actually felt by those individuals who experienced them.

One of the difficulties in writing about the Holocaust is that the reader is unable to identify with great masses of people. We can certainly comprehend and feel aghast at the ghoulish facts presented by the historian. But as individuals ourselves we can reach out imaginatively only towards the experience of other individuals. As Nora Levin writes:

> the Holocaust refuses to go the way of most history . . . because the events surrounding it are in a very real sense incomprehensible . . . Ordinary human beings simply cannot rethink themselves into such a world and ordinary ways to achieve empathy fail. . . . The world of Auschwitz was, in truth, another planet.[1]

Yet this is where imaginative writing scores over historical writing. Its proximity to the *feel* of events or situations brings us as close as it is possible to get to this other planet. And as in all tragedy, one particular figure, one specific situation, can represent the many. Literature may have a number of other functions too, but in letting the reader *into* a representative situation, experience, or historical period, it is supreme. As Aristotle pointed out, literature has more to tell us about truth than historical narrative has.

Many powerful prose works have been widely published on the subject of the Holocaust. They have been variously classified as memoirs, diaries, records, novels, although it may be questioned whether such sharp distinctions are worth drawing in this context. Drama too has emerged from this same source. Yet the poetry which has arisen and forced itself from the pens of many authors of various backgrounds, different standpoints and a variety of languages has nowhere else been gathered together in as focused and representative a collection as this, enabling the reader to reach for them in one convenient compilation.

While representative, this volume nevertheless has had to be selective rather than comprehensive if for no other reason than lack of space. (There are some well-known poets in this field who have had to be left out altogether, such as Uri Zwi Greenberg and the poet of the ghetto, Itzchak Katzenelson.) Even so, as editor, I have had three overall considerations in mind in selecting poems from a wide spectrum of possibilities.

The first was that the poems on the subject of the Holocaust here included had to be of literary merit in themselves, and be well translated where applicable. That is to say, the translation had not only to be accurate, but had also to constitute an autonomous poem in its new language.

Secondly, I have tried to include as wide a variety of poets writing from as many divergent perspectives within the Holocaust maelstrom as space would permit. Not all anthologists are guided by this principle but prefer to present fewer poets at greater length. I did not think this would serve the purpose of this collection. For instance, it would not have shown the diversity of victims of the Holocaust. Of couse, as is well known, numerically it was mainly the Jews of Europe who were overwhelmingly affected by the Holocaust. But it is well to remember that this was not exclusively so.[2] While the authorities at the Auschwitz Museum in Poland are only just beginning to come to terms with the former fact, many writers in the West are only now starting to take account of the latter.[3]

My third consideration has been to lend some order to the plethora of poetic responses to the Holocaust by organizing the poems into subsections of theme and application. This is reflected in the chapter divisions. While some poems belong squarely in one particular section, others could easily be placed in two or more different chapter divisions, while yet others may be deemed to belong outside these sections altogether. My arrangement then is intended to suggest a helpful framework for the reader's involvement, rather than to impose an arbitrary categorization.

For the first three chapter headings I have followed the contours of the Holocaust process. This began with the deliberate alienation of ethnic minorities. From the beginning, throughout Europe, wherever Hitler's impact began to make itself felt, those people whom he picked out as being his particular aversion, in the main Jews, began to feel alienated both psychologically and physically from their host culture. The fact that Jewish communities had been living in Germany, as elsewhere in central Europe, since the Middle Ages at least was ignored. Soon they were made to feel unwanted, outsiders (many placards in the streets and in shops proclaimed them as public enemies), gradually cast off from society, whether from their jobs, their schools and colleges, or their equally indigenous cultural traditions. Their own quiet, stable, traditional mode of living was thoroughly disturbed, their sense of identity radically undermined. This was registered perhaps most acutely by those who were children at the time, with a child's close observation and indelibly retentive memory. In some cases it was not until decades later and in other countries that these impressions and traumas issued in poems that sprang forth with all their repressed pain and energy. (See for example the poems of Karen Gershon or Lotte Kramer.)

The next stage events took was that of active persecution. Active anti-Semitism under the perverted but infectious ravings of Julius Streicher and the more sophisticated vicious outpourings of Goebbels became widespread. People who were Jews were not only shunned and jeered at, but frequently forced out of their homes, driven out of their country, sometimes to hang about at frontiers where no one would accept them, their belongings confiscated, their civil rights annulled. (A similar process is now called 'ethnic cleansing' by the Serbs instead of 'Judenrein' by the Nazis.) Those who still remained in their homes and had been comfortably off beforehand began to live on their savings which rapidly became depleted. Those who were poor from the start became poorer. There was less food, and in the ghettoes of the East for some eventually none at all. They literally starved to death. See Ficowski's poem 'A girl of six from the ghetto begging in Smolna Street in 1942'. Throughout Nazi-occupied Europe the process repeated itself in principle, though the sequence or details differed to some degree. Fathers might be dragged away to a detention camp or for slave labour. Sometimes they returned. Others were deported. No one knew what had become of them. Some families would be told to leave town, others torn apart. Where were they to go? What did the future hold?

> At night and in the wind and the rain
> we're whirled on the roads,
> in the parks, on steps and stations,
> like masses of leaves

wrote Chaim Grade in his poem 'Refugees'. Can we enter into this anxiety, this not knowing what to do, where to hide? It would indeed be strange if there were no poems written about these and similar circumstances. (See other poets such as David Vogel or Bertolt Brecht.)

However, perhaps the strongest and certainly the most numerous poems on the Holocaust are those that refer to the actual process of destruction which chronologically constitutes the next phase of the Holocaust process. These poems emanate from many writers, Jews and non-Jews alike, and in many languages. Countless individual people, like any one of us now reading these pages, were collected like vermin and destroyed in any number of different ways, not only in the death camps themselves but also through the systematic shootings, the live pit-burnings, and partisan trench warfare. (See the poems of János Pilinszky, Miklós Radnóti, and later in a rare case of German self-destruction, Peter Huchel's 'Roads'.) One of the most remarkable and well-known poems on this theme is

'Babii Yar' by Yevgeny Yevtushenko in which he, a Russian non-combatant, and of a later generation, pays homage by personally identifying with the many thousands of Jews who were slaughtered by the Germans in a ravine at Babii Yar, in the Ukraine. In solidarity he writes,

> I am
>> each old man
>>> here shot dead.
> I am
>> every child
>>> here shot dead.
> Nothing in me
>> shall ever forget!

Those who actually witnessed such barely describable scenes and escaped with their lives are often driven to write of them in verse of great intensity even though they themselves may not be natural poets. See the poem 'Shipment to Maidanek' by the survivor Ephraim Fogel in which, with great restraint and tragic irony, he depicts the activities at the death camp of Maidanek, near Lublin in Poland, where human beings were regarded and treated as inanimate objects to be carefully and systematically sorted out like boxes of goods and, Germanlike, efficiently disposed of. Yet important writers or not, their indelible memories, their intensity of suffering, their moral incomprehension, their spiritual outrage, make significant poets of them all, whether they write in an apparently simple style or in a more sophisticated one. Compare and contrast, for example, 'I Keep Forgetting' by the 'second-generation' Lily Brett, and 'Death Fugue' by Paul Celan, himself a former camp inmate. But perhaps most astonishing of all from the point of view of variety of perspective is a poem called 'The Sun of Auschwitz'. For even from within this closed-off, infernal *universe concentrationaire*, from this 'other planet', comes a poem of incredible tenderness and elegiac lyricism by Tadeusz Borowski, an erstwhile prisoner in Auschwitz, who survived to write his terrifying and wonderful prose account, *This Way for the Gas, Ladies and Gentlemen*, before committing suicide six years after his liberation. Looking out from this compound of death and horror, he spoke of the person he loved there and of the

> green of the distant meadows, lightly
> lifted to the clouds by birds . . .
> your smile as elusive
> as a shade of the colour of the wind,
> a leaf trembling on the edge
> of sun and shadow, fleeting
> yet always there. So you are
> for me today, in the seagreen
> sky, the greenery and
> the leaf-rustling wind . . .

And are we to leave out of account the other side of the coin of this kingdom of malevolence, namely the terrible suffering of some of those who directly or indirectly brought about the Holocaust? See Van K. Brock's 'Remembering Dresden' or Michael Hamburger's 'Between the Lines'.

Afterwards, when Nazi Germany was defeated and civilization was presumed to be going to continue, some people asked what it could *mean* to write 'a poem' any more. After a highly cultured nation such as Germany could descend into such an abyss of barbarism, how could one continue to talk blithely of 'culture', of artistic forms, of art, of beauty as though nothing had disturbed the value and significance of such discourse, a discourse which itself had emanated from this very same traditional, highly wrought 'culture' that had brought this inferno about. After this inner failure of civilization, art was seen as hollow, at best existing in a moral vacuum. Then what could the ontological status of a poem *be* after Auschwitz? How could poetic language itself be anything but superficial, irrelevant, marginal in a world of such horror since language was incommensurate to express it? How on earth could the poet simply revert to the old notions of order, form, symmetry, verbal felicity as though nothing had altered our perceptions of the real? To do this would be mere escapism; fundamentally such writing would be gibberish, without meaning, no more than kitsch. Beauty was *not* truth, as Keats had averred, nor was truth beauty. Neither was there any equation or even interaction between it and goodness. Symmetry was a lie, harmony was a lie. For within such notions how were we to accommodate for example Himmler's notorious speech at Posen to his nefarious SS officers on 4 October 1943 when he urged them not to become downhearted or to weary of their slaughtering assignments, but to remember that in pursuing them they were in effect writing a glorious page of German history, even if it were a page that nevertheless could not actually be printed. What could the poet say here, now, with this obscenity before him? What poetic forms, what poetic images, what language was adequate to deal with a world in which such an ideology had become all-pervasive? Evil had become good, good evil.

We are living in Biblical times

writes William Heyen in his poem 'Passover – the Injections'.

In 1949, Theodor Adorno, a leading German critic, aghast at what had happened, coined an expression that was to have immense influence and long-term repercussions. 'Nach Auschwitz,' he wrote, 'ein Gedicht zu schreiben, ist barbarisch'[4] (After Auschwitz it is barbaric to write poetry). While amongst critics this silence-inducing precept became seminal (Michael Hamburger points out in *The Truth of Poetry* , 1969, that writing poems after Auschwitz, by then a symbol as well as the name of an actual concentration camp, now became 'a taboo'), fortunately it was not altogether effective amongst a number of actual poets, otherwise we should not now have the works of Paul Celan, Primo Levi, Elie Wiesel and many others. Nevertheless, at the time, Adorno's outburst of rage, pain and indignation towards a culture that had gone so castastrophically awry, seemed both just and somehow consoling. Indeed what sort of value could one ascribe to a 'culture' in which there seemed no incongruity in a situation where the Jewish musicians of Auschwitz were allowed to go on living on condition that they could bring themselves to play the works of Beethoven and Schubert to SS units who earlier in the day had been systematically gassing their fellow human beings?

Such an obscene contradiction, Adorno was saying, was too great to integrate into any kind of traditional 'culture'. How could any person of conscience, of feeling, of spiritual and – yes, cultural – awareness go on writing 'beautiful' verses as though nothing had happened to change our perception of reality, of the function of language, when the whole vault of the heavens still echoed to the stifled cries of those many millions who had perished in such infernal circumstances? What *was* a poem any more? What *was* beauty any more? In a different context Yeats proclaimed a *new* beauty had to be born. Shostakovitch in his Thirteenth Symphony, based on the atrocities committed at Babii Yar, attempted to bring this about: a beauty expressive of horror. But for many others, as Adorno encouraged, silence alone was possible. Speechlessness alone could reflect integrity. To seek to portray reality with inadequate words would betray that reality and the voiceless dead at its core. The great Polish poet, Tadeusz Różewicz grappled with this issue even, paradoxically, within his poems. In his poem 'In the Midst of Life' he tries to reuse simple words, words which needed to be reborn in order to signify meaning yet once more.

After the end of the world
after death
I found myself in the midst of life
creating myself
building life
people animals landscapes

this is a table I said
this is a table
there is bread and a knife on the table . . .

For, counterbalanced against silence was another impulse: to bear witness. To say nothing might be the most dignified stance to adopt but, as it is said, nothing shall come of nothing. Jerzy Ficowski, working on this dilemma in his poem 'The Execution of Memory' writes,

> I would like just to be silent
> but being silent I lie.

To remain silent would surely only compound the evil. It would be forgotten, together with the murdered millions whose voices were stilled for ever. Even in the ghettos (in the camps it was impossible) the urge to write, to portray their incremental agony day after day, was overwhelmingly urgent for those who were able to wield a pen. 'Record, record,' urged Emanuel Ringelblum feverishly as he sat at his table in the Warsaw ghetto, pen in hand, hungry and cold, knowing that his death was near. People often buried their writing so that it would be preserved. No philosophy, however persuasive, in the end can legislate silence. Speech after suffering is an ultimately indestructible human trait, a quintessential human gift however inadequate.

And so after the maelstrom itself had abated, from 1945 onwards, gradually those who remained above the earth found a voice. Slowly their work trickled through to a stunned and paralysed world. It is only now, 50 years later, that this trickle has grown to a flood. As for them, the survivors, in 'What Luck', Różewicz speaks for them all when he opens his eyes from the nightmare behind him and looks out with a sense of profound blessing upon the smallest specks of normality reforming themselves around him. 'What luck,' he writes,

> What luck I can pick
> berries in the wood
> I thought
> there is no wood no berries.

What luck I can lie
in the shade of a tree
I thought trees
no longer give shade.

What luck I am with you
my heart beats so
I thought man
has no heart.

Writing poems was still somehow possible.

This collection ranges from poems which, at one end of the spectrum, fall within the Biblical tradition of Lamentations, and at the other end, contains poems of appealing simplicity and directness. (See Primo Levi's powerful 'Shemá' or Paul Celan's 'Psalm' or 'The Jugs', and the slight and touching anonymous 'I Believe'.) Here, as in Elie Wiesel's 'Ani Maamin', are poems which profoundly address the notion of the divine, and man's grappling with the problem of evil. In Wiesel's book *Night* someone in the crowd asks 'Where is God now?' as the SS are hanging a small boy in the main square at Auschwitz while the prisoners are made to stand around to attention and watch. He is there, someone replies, on that tree and in that noose.

One poem pays tribute to those rare people of pure goodness who rescued the hunted at the potential cost of their own lives. (See Abraham Sutzkever's '1980' in which, hidden in a cellar and fed by a simple peasant woman, he describes how he recognized his rescuer's identity by her coded footstep in the snow.) Yet other poems portray harrowing scenes, perhaps from memory or another's record, such as Randall Jarrell's 'In the Camp There Was One Alive' or Charles Reznikoff's narrative poem based on documentary evidence but conveyed with spare yet vivid immediacy, and without comment. Sylvia Plath's celebrated poem 'Daddy' is included because it embodies an instance where Holocaust imagery abounds, some might say is exploited, in the service, not of the Holocaust itself, but of the poet's parental vendetta, showing how Holocaust terms have become absorbed in everyday language. There are even two humorous poems: see Magnus Enzenberger's 'Portrait of a House Detective' and Anna Swirszczynska's 'He Was Lucky'.

Naturally, not all the poems included are of equal literary distinction, and some even challenge accepted moral views, such as Denise Levertov's controversial poem on Adolf Eichmann. Nevertheless, they have earned their place on account of their unusual approach or perspective. Together they enable us to become involved in Holocaust poetry within a broader framework.

With this compilation of poems we commemorate the dead and salute with love and with pride all those men, women, and the one and a half million children who perished so brutally in the Holocaust epoch. History will only repeat itself unless we can accommodate the knowledge that they perished, not through some impersonal stroke of fate, or because all mankind is imperfect and equally to blame, but through the deliberate acts of specific men and women throughout Europe and beyond, all of whom had a choice, however minimal, to do otherwise.

This is a book to mourn with, to weep with, to show solidarity with, perhaps to pray with. For us Jews it offers an opportunity to recover more fully that part of our heritage which the paralysis of pain has prevented us from making more fully our own until this time of grace.

Endnotes
1 *The Holocaust*, N.Y. 1968, pp. xi–xii.
2 As Elie Wiesel has pointed out, 'While not all victims were Jews, all Jews were [intended] victims', Preface to *Report to the President*, Washington, 1979, p. iii.
3 See *A Mosaic of Victims, Non-Jews Persecuted and Murdered by the Nazis*, edited by Michael Berenbaum, 1990, and *The Other Victims*, by Ina R. Friedman, Boston, 1990.
4 *Gesellschaftstheorie und Kulturkritik*, Suhrkamp Verlag, Frankfurt a.M., 1975, p. 65.

The Poems

Alienation

Heritage

The ram came last of all. And Abraham
did not know that it came to answer the
boy's question* – first of his strength
when his day was on the wane.

The old man raised his head. Seeing
that it was no dream and that the angel
stood there – the knife slipped from his hand.

The boy, released from his bonds,
saw his father's back.

Isaac, as the story goes, was not
sacrificed. He lived for many years,
saw what pleasure had to offer,
until his eyesight dimmed.

But he bequeathed that hour to his offspring.
They are born with a knife in their hearts.

Hayim Gouri

---

* In Genesis 22:7 Isaac says, 'Here are the fire and the wood, but where is the
young beast for the sacrifice?'

Europe, Late

Violins float in the sky,
and a straw hat. I beg your pardon,
what year is it?
Thirty-nine and a half, still awfully early,
you can turn off the radio.
I would like to introduce you to:
the sea breeze, the life of the party,
terribly mischievous,
whirling in a bell-skirt, slapping down
the worried newspapers: tango! tango!
And the park hums to itself:
    I kiss your dainty hand, madame,
    your hand as soft and elegant
    as a white suede glove. You'll see, madame,
    that everything will be all right,
    just heavenly – you wait and see.
    No it could never happen here,
    don't worry so – you'll see – it could

Dan Pagis
(Translated by Stephen Mitchell)

The Shoemaker's Wife

She came to us walking, at night.
Our bundle of mended shoes
Hot secrets in her shopping bag.

By the door in the hall she stood
And cried. Her autumn hair
Wild from the wind.

Her red-blue eyes like
Sores in her face,
Sad postmarks

From the cobbler's shop
In the narrow old town
Where her husband hammered

And stitched his days;
Where the sign 'No Jews'
Newly pinned to the door

Pleased her sons'
Keen suspicion
That mastered all our lives.

Lotte Kramer

The Burning of the Books

When the Regime commanded that books with harmful knowledge
Should be publicly burned on all sides
Oxen were forced to drag cart loads of books
To the bonfires, a banished
Writer, one of the best, scanning the list of the
Burned, was shocked to find that his
Books had been passed over. He rushed to his desk
On wings of wrath, and wrote a letter to those in power.
Burn me! he wrote with flying pen, burn me. Haven't my books
Always reported the truth? And here you are
Treating me like a liar! I command you:
Burn me!

Bertolt Brecht
(Translated by John Willet)

First They Came for the Jews

First they came for the Jews
and I did not speak out
because I was not a Jew.
Then they came for the Communists
and I did not speak out
because I was not a Communist.
Then they came for the trade unionists
and I did not speak out
because I was not a trade unionist.
Then they came for me
and there was no one left
to speak out for me.

Pastor Niemöller

A Footnote Extended

for Thomas Szasz's *Karl Kraus and the Soul Doctors*

Dr Szasz, professor, sir,
I read your book.
I won't make criticisms (I could)
but more attention, please,
for Egon Friedman,
born in Vienna, 1878,
of Jewish parents.

Who, insulted, endured.
Who studied in Berlin,
later in Heidelberg:
studied German
studied philosophy
studied natural science;
did not write a treatise
on the whale,
that hunted mammal
posing as a fish.

But returned to Vienna,
changed his visiting card.
Friedell now, not Friedman.
'Hello Dr Friedell,
you're a mensch, Dr Friedell.
Here's a bowl of wax apples,
here's a vase of paper flowers,
here's margarine in a lordly dish.'

He ignored such tauntings.
Tall, he turned the other cheek,
he converted to Christianity –
defended the Gospel
against Mosaic subversion;
attacked the Jewish Science
of Psychoanalysis,
called its practitioners –
Freud, Abraham, Stekel –
'underground blood-suckers'.

Ah, applause now
for the proselyte
so soon to be successful,
so edgily celebrated
under the probing, chalky
spotlight of cabaret-actor,
writer, critic, author of
Cultural History of the Modern Age.

When the Nazis marched
into Austria
– strange amphigouri
of circumstance –
Friedell, in his bachelor room,
walked towards the long mirror,
saw Friedman approaching.
Whispered Friedman,
screamed FRIEDMAN,
and killed himself.

Dannie Abse

Refugee Blues

Say this city has ten million souls,
Some are living in mansions, some are living in holes:
Yet there's no place for us, my dear, yet there's no place for us.

Once we had a country and we thought it fair,
Look in the atlas and you'll find it there:
We cannot go there now, my dear, we cannot go there now.

In the village churchyard there grows an old yew,
Every spring it blossoms anew:
Old passports can't do that, my dear, old passports can't do
    that.

The consul banged the table and said,
'If you've got no passport you're officially dead':
But we are still alive, my dear, but we are still alive.

Went to a committee; they offered me a chair;
Asked me politely to return next year:
But where shall we go today, my dear, but where shall we go
    today?

Came to a public meeting; the speaker got up and said:
'If we let them in, they will steal our daily bread':
He was talking of you and me, my dear, he was talking of you
    and me.

Thought I heard the thunder rumbling in the sky;
It was Hitler over Europe, saying 'They must die':
O we were in his mind, my dear, O we were in his mind.

Saw a poodle in a jacket fastened with a pin,
Saw a door opened and a cat let in:
But they weren't German Jews, my dear, but they weren't
    German Jews.

Went down the harbour and stood upon the quay,
Saw the fish swimming as if they were free:
Only ten feet away, my dear, only ten feet away.

Walked through a wood, saw the birds in the trees;
They had no politicians and sang at their ease:
They weren't the human race, my dear, they weren't the
    human race.

Dreamed I saw a building with a thousand floors,
A thousand windows and a thousand doors:
Not one of them was ours, my dear, not one of them was ours.

Stood on a great plain in the falling snow;
Ten thousand soldiers marched to and fro:
Looking for you and me, my dear, looking for you and me.

March 1939
W. H. Auden

How Can I See You, Love

How can I see you, love,
Standing alone
Amid storms of grief
Without feeling my heart shake?

A deep night,
Blacker than the blackness of your eyes,
Has fallen silently
On the world

And is touching your curls.

Come,
My hand will clasp your dreaming
Hand,
And I shall lead you between the nights,

Through the pale mists of childhood,
As my father once guided me
To the house of prayer.

David Vogel
(Translated by A. C. Jacobs)

Persecution

1940

Fleeing from my fellow-countrymen
I have now reached Finland. Friends
Whom yesterday I didn't know, put up some beds
In clean rooms. Over the radio
I hear victory bulletins of the scum of the earth. Curiously
I examine a map of the continent. High up in Lapland
Towards the Arctic Ocean
I can still see a small door.

Bertolt Brecht
(Translated by John Willet)

The Red Cross Telegram

The Red Cross telegram
Read when it came
Those five and twenty words;
The terror, fear,
Was there; I did not dare
To grasp the cruelty
That now I know
It did contain:
'We have to move,
Our residence will not
Remain this town,
Farewell, beloved child.'

How can I ever sing
A requiem
In silent, dark despair,
Transfiguring
Your calvary of nails
And gas and graves.

Lotte Kramer

The German Frontier at Basel:
1942 & 1992

Just four miles to go and the frontier ahead,
A few miles ahead and the weather ideal.
A soft hanging haze over wooded landscape,
Trees on the turn yet the air warm and dry.
Peacefully at mid-day golden stretches
Of new-mown fields lie open and benign.
A cooling breeze sweeps the grassy slopes.
Early autumn: Tabernacles, Harvest Festival.

Disaster could not strike on a day
Such as this. His papers, after all,
Were in perfect order. His directions
Clear, his plan foolproof. Some food
Stowed away, sufficient cash. No parcels
Or dependents. Just himself with a small,
A really modest sized suitcase. Stop worrying,
He told himself. You're one of the lucky ones.

Only the tell-tale burn in the stomach,
The deliberate effort to relax tense muscles.
Short of breath. Much thirst. Little energy.
At the border at last, he did, he didn't
Expect the difficulties. He was, he wasn't
Prepared for the arrest. He did, he didn't
Anticipate the arrangements: the jam-packed trains,
The sweat, the stench, the gas, the horror.

~

Today as then, only reversing the directions,
The harvest is in, the fields as peaceful.
Just four miles to go and the frontier ahead:
An invisible line, an unguarded signpost.
Yet fear grips his gut, and anguish and anger:
The black-clad figures, the brutal voices,
The crowded cattle-trucks, the reeking odour,
The sweat, the stench, the gas, the horror.

Hilda Schiff

He Was Lucky

The old man
leaves his house, carries books.
A German soldier snatches his books
flings them in the mud.

The old man picks them up,
the soldier hits him in the face.
The old man falls,
the soldier kicks him and walks away.

The old man
lies in mud and blood.
Under him he feels
the books.

Anna Swirszczynska
(Translated by Magnus J. Krynski &
Robert A. Maguire)

I Saw My Father Drowning

I saw my father drowning
In surging days.
His weak hand gave a last white flutter
In the distance –
And he was gone.

I kept on alone
Along the shore,
A boy still,
With small, thin legs,
And have grown as far as this.

And now I am my father,
And all those waves
Have broken over me,
And left my soul numb.

But all I held dear
Have gone into the wilderness
And I can stretch out a hand to no one.

I am happy to rest
In the black cradle of night,
Under the sky's canopy,
Studded with silver.

David Vogel
(Translated by A. C. Jacobs)

There Is a Last, Solitary Coach

There is a last, solitary coach about to leave.
Let us get in and go,
For it won't wait.

I have seen young girls going softly
With sad faces
That looked ashamed and sorry
Like purple sunsets,

And chubby, pink children
Who went simply
Because they were called.

And I've seen men
Who stepped proud and straight through the world's streets,
Whose large eyes went ranging
Far and wide,
They too got in calmly
And left.

And we are the last.
Day is declining.
The last, solitary coach is about to leave.
Let us too get in quietly
And go,
For it won't wait.

David Vogel
(Translated by A. C. Jacobs)

Clouded Sky

The moon hangs on a clouded sky.
I am surprised that I live.
Anxiously and with great care, death looks for us
and those it finds are all terribly white.

Sometimes a year looks back and howls
then drops to its knees.
Autumn is too much for me. It waits again
and winter waits with its dull pain.

The forest bleeds. The hours bleed.
Time spins overhead
and the wind scrawls
big dark numbers on the snow.

But I am still here
and I know why and why the air feels heavy –
a warm silence full of tiny noises circles me
just as it was before my birth.

I stop at the foot of a tree,
Its leaves cry with anger.
A branch reaches down. Is it strangling me?
I am not a coward. I am not weak, I am

tired. And silent. And the branch
is also mute and afraid as it enters my hair.
I should forget it, but I
forget nothing.

Clouds pour across the moon. Anger
leaves a poisonous dark-green bruise on the sky.
I roll myself a cigarette,
slowly, carefully. I live.

June 8, 1940.   *Miklós Radnóti*
                        (Translated by Steven Polgar, S. Berg &
                                      S. J. Marks)

The Butterfly

He was the last. Truly the last.
Such yellowness was bitter and blinding
Like the sun's tear shattered on stone.
That was his true colour.
And how easily he climbed, and how high,
Certainly, climbing, he wanted
To kiss the last of my world.

I have been here for seven weeks,
'Ghettoized'.
Who loved me have found me,
Daisies call to me,
And the branches also of the white chestnut in the yard.
But I haven't seen a butterfly here.
That last one was the last one.
There are no butterflies, here, in the ghetto.

Pavel Friedmann,
Theresienstadt, 4 June 1942.

Elegy

in honour of the Warsaw Ghetto uprising, April 19, 1943

No more, no more Jewish townships in Poland,
In Hrubieszcrow, Karczew, Brody, Falenica.
Vainly would you look for lighted candles in windows,
And listen for chanting from a wooden synagogue.

The last scourings, the Jewish rags have vanished,
They sprinkled sand over the blood, swept away the footprints
And whitewashed the walls with bluish lime,
Like after a plague or for a great feast day.

One moon shines here, cool, pale, alien,
Nowadays my kinsmen, the bardic Jewish boys,
Will not find outside the town, on the highway, when the
   night lights up
The two gold moons of Chagall.

Those moons are now orbiting another planet,
They have flown away, frightened by the grim silence.
They are no more, these townships where the cobbler
   was a poet,
The watchmaker a philosopher, the barber a troubadour.

No longer does the wind weave the old Hebraic theme
with Polish airs and Slavonic pain:
those villages and orchards
where old Jews still mourned Holy Jerusalem.

They are no more, these townships, they passed like a shadow
And this shadow shall lie across our words,
Till they embrace like brothers and join anew,
Two nations which supped full of the same suffering.

Antoni Slonimski
(Translated by Isaac Komen)

A Cartload of Shoes

The wheels hurry onward, onward.
What do they carry?
They carry a cartload
Of shivering shoes.

The wagon like a canopy
in the evening light;
The shoes – clustered
Like people in a dance.

A wedding, a holiday?
Has something blinded my eyes?
The shoes – I seem
To recognize them.

The heels go tapping
With a clatter and a din.
From our old Vilna streets
They drive us to Berlin.

I should not ask
But something tears at my tongue
Shoes, tell me the truth
Where are they, the feet?

The feet from those boots
With button like dew –
And here, where is the body
And there, where is the bride?

Where is the child
To fill those shoes
Why has the bride
Gone barefoot?

Through the slippers and the boots
I see those my mother used to wear
She kept them for the Sabbath
Her favourite pair.

And the heels go tapping:
With a clatter and a din,
From our old Vilna streets
They drive us to Berlin.

Abraham Sutzkever
(Translated by David G. Roskies)

How?

How will you fill your goblet
On the day of liberation? And with what?
Are you prepared, in your joy, to endure
The dark keening you have heard
Where skulls of days glitter
In a bottomless pit?

You will search for a key to fit
Your jammed locks. You will bite
The sidewalks like bread,
Thinking: It used to be better.
And time will gnaw at you like a cricket
Caught in a fist.

Then your memory will resemble
An ancient buried town.
And your estranged eyes will burrow down
Like a mole, a mole. . . .

Abraham Sutzkever
Vilna Ghetto,
February 14, 1943
(Translated by Chana Bloch)

How They Killed My Grandmother

How did they kill my grandmother?
This is how they killed my grandmother:
In the morning a tank
Rolled up to the city bank.

One hundred and fifty Jews of the town,
Weightless
            from a whole year's starvation,
Pale,
     with the pangs of death upon them,
Came there, carrying bundles.
Polizei and young German soldiers
Cheerfully herded the old men and old women,
And led them, clanking with pots and pans,
Led them
        far out of town.

But my diminutive grandmother, Lilliputian,
My seventy-year-old grandmother,
Swore at the Germans,
Cursed like a trooper,

Yelled at them where I was.
She cried: 'My grandson's at the front.
Just you dare
Lay hands on me.
Those are our guns
          that you hear, Boche!'

Grandmother wept and shouted
And walked.
                    And then started
Shouting again.
From every window rose a din.
Ivanovs and Andreyevnas leant down,
Sidorovnas and Petrovnas wept:

'Keep it up, Polina Matveyevna!
You just show them. Give it them straight!'
They clamoured:
                    'What's there to be so scared
About this German enemy!'
And so they decided to kill my grandmother,
While they were still passing through the town.

A bullet kicked up her hair.
A grey lock floated down,
And my grandmother fell to the ground.
That's how they did it to her.

Boris Slutsky
(Translated by Daniel Weissbort)

from Holocaust

When the Second World War began
he was living in Lodz with his mother.
The family was hungry
and his mother became bloated from hunger –
as many were.
His mother and her family escaped from the ghetto in Lodz
and fled to the Warsaw ghetto;
but there it became much worse:
his mother had sold everything she had
and they had nothing to eat.
She then told him to get to the Lublin area
where other members of the family lived,
and he escaped to a small town.

One morning he heard cries and shrieking:
the Germans were taking the Jews to the market place.
They crowded them into freight cars
and he was among them.
There was hardly room to stand
and many fainted.
But the journey took only two or three hours
and they were brought to a death camp.
When they got off the train
they were hurried to a small gate,
the SS men shouting, 'Hurry! Hurry!'
and there the men were taken from the women and children.
While this was going on
a band was playing.

The men stayed there all night
but the women and children were taken at once to the gas
　　chambers.
Many of the Jews had not believed there would be any mass
　　extermination –
a few murders, of course;
and even when they were jammed into the freight cars,
many were happy not to be going to a camp they knew to be a
　　hard labour camp
and going eastward instead:
it had been rumoured that they would be taken to the Ukraine
　　to work in the fields
now that Germany had taken over most of it.
But some remembered a Jew who had come to town and said:
'Do not believe what you are told.
The Jews are not being taken to the Ukraine;
they are sent to death camps –
and killed there.'
But nobody believed him;
they thought he was just trying to start a panic.
And even in the camp they had now been sent to –
a few hundred feet from the gas chambers –
the men were told by the Germans that in a few weeks they
　　would rejoin their families.
They saw the belongings of the women and children piled up;
but the Germans said:
'They are getting new clothes.
You are going to be gathered together and then sent to the
　　Ukraine.'

•　•　•

There were really three camps at that camp:
one for shoemakers, tailors, and other craftsmen;
another for those who worked at sorting the clothes of those
    who came in the transports and were gassed;
and the third camp where the gas chambers were.
The morning after the arrival of the Jewish men who had just
    come,
the Germans began to sort them:
choosing the young and able-bodied by saying, 'du' – the
    German familiar for 'you'.
In about half an hour most of the men who had come in that
    transport
had been taken to the gas chambers
and only about a hundred and fifty were left to work;
the young man who had fled from Warsaw to the Lublin area
    among them.

He was put to work taking and piling up the clothing of the
    people who had come –
and were coming – in the transports
and kept seeing that many who had come disappeared.
After the young man had worked for a while the first day,
he was dazed
and as he stood, dazed and benumbed –
he was only fifteen then –
a Jew came up to him and said, 'My boy, if you are going to
    behave this way, you are not going to survive here.'

• • •

After the Jew who had recognized the man from his
   home town
had been working in the woods for some time,
other Jews from his own town were among the dead
and among them –
his wife and his two children!
He lay down next to his wife and children and wanted the
   Germans to shoot him;
but one of the SS men said:
'You still have enough strength to work,'
and pushed him away.
That evening he tried to hang himself
but his friends in the cellar would not let him
and said, 'As long as your eyes are open,
there is hope.'
The next day the man who had tried to die was on a truck.

They were still in the woods
and he asked one of the SS men for a cigarette.
He himself did not smoke usually
but he lit the cigarette and, when he was back where his
   companions were sitting, said:
'Look here! He gives out cigarettes.
Why don't you all ask him for a cigarette?'
They all got up –
they were in the back of the truck –
and went forwards
and he was left behind.
He had a little knife
and made a slit in the tarpaulin at the side
and jumped out;
came down on his knees
but got up and ran.
By the time the SS men began shooting
he was gone in the woods.

Charles Reznikoff

The Assumption of Miriam from the Street in the Winter of 1942

snowflakes were teeming down
the sky was collapsing in shreds

so she was being assumed
she passed unmoving
whiteness after whiteness
mild height
after height
in an elija's chariot
of degradation

above the fallen angels
of snows
into a zenith of frost
higher and higher and
hosanna
lifted
right to the bottom

Jerzy Ficowski
(Translated by Keith Bosley)

Destruction

(i)

Death Fugue

Black milk of daybreak we drink it at sundown
we drink it at noon in the morning we drink it at night
we drink and we drink it
we dig a grave in the breezes there one lies unconfined
A man lives in the house he plays with the serpents he writes
he writes when dusk falls to Germany your golden hair
    Margarete
he writes it and steps out of doors and the stars are flashing he
    whistles his pack out
he whistles his Jews out in earth has them dig for a grave
he commands us strike up for the dance

Black milk of daybreak we drink you at night
we drink in the morning at noon we drink you at sundown
we drink and we drink you
A man lives in the house he plays with the serpents he writes
he writes when dusk falls to Germany your golden hair
    Margarete
your ashen hair Shulamith we dig a grave in the breezes there
    one lies unconfined

He calls out jab deeper into the earth you lot you others sing
    now and play
he grabs at the iron in his belt he waves it his eyes are blue
jab deeper you lot with your spades you others play on for the
    dance

Black milk of daybreak we drink you at night
we drink you at noon in the morning we drink you at
    sundown
we drink and we drink you
a man lives in the house your golden hair Margarete
your ashen hair Shulamith he plays with the serpents

He calls out more sweetly play death death is a master from
    Germany
he calls out more darkly now stroke your strings then as
    smoke you will rise into air
then a grave you will have in the clouds there one lies
    unconfined

Black milk of daybreak we drink you at night
we drink you at noon death is a master from Germany
we drink you at sundown and in the morning we drink and
    we drink you
death is a master from Germany his eyes are blue
he strikes you with leaden bullets his aim is true
a man lives in the house your golden hair Margarete
he sets his pack on to us he grants us a grave in the air
he plays with the serpents and daydreams death is a master
    from Germany

your golden hair Margarete
your ashen hair Shulamith

Paul Celan
(Translated by Michael Hamburger)

O the Chimneys

And though after my skin worms destroy this
body, yet in my flesh shall I see God. JOB 19:26

O the chimneys
On the ingeniously devised habitations of death
When Israel's body drifted as smoke
Through the air –
Was welcomed by a star, a chimney sweep,
A star that turned black
Or was it a ray of sun?

O the chimneys!
Freedomway for Jeremiah and Job's dust –
Who devised you and laid stone upon stone
The road for refugees of smoke?

O the habitations of death,
Invitingly appointed
For the host who used to be a guest –
O you fingers
Laying the threshold
Like a knife between life and death –

O you chimneys,
O you fingers
And Israel's body as smoke through the air!

Nelly Sachs
(Translated by Michael Hamburger)

Never Shall I Forget

Never shall I forget that night,
the first night in the camp
which has turned my life into one long night,
seven times cursed and seven times sealed.

Never shall I forget that smoke.
Never shall I forget the little faces of the children
whose bodies I saw turned into wreaths of smoke
beneath a silent blue sky.

Never shall I forget those flames
which consumed my faith for ever.
Never shall I forget that nocturnal silence
which deprived me for all eternity of the desire to live.

Never shall I forget those moments
which murdered my God and my soul
and turned my dreams to dust.

Never shall I forget these things,
even if I am condemned to live
as long as God Himself.

Never.

Elie Wiesel

Testimony

No no: they definitely were
human beings: uniforms, boots.
How to explain? They were created
in the image.

I was a shade.
A different creator made me.

And he in his mercy left nothing of me that would die.
And I fled to him, rose weightless, blue,
forgiving – I would even say: apologizing –
smoke to omnipotent smoke
without image or likeness.

Dan Pagis
(Translated by Stephen Mitchell)

The Roll Call

He stands, stamps a little in his boots,
rubs his hands. He's cold in the morning breeze:
a diligent angel, who has worked hard for his promotions.
Suddenly he thinks he's made a mistake: all eyes,
he counts again in the open notebook
all the bodies waiting for him in the square,
camp within camp: only I
am not there, am not there, am a mistake,
turn off my eyes, quickly, erase my shadow.
I shall not want. The sum will be in order
without me: here for eternity.

Dan Pagis
(Translated by Stephen Mitchell)

Be Seeing You

After the third evening round
In the yard of the concentration camp
We disperse to our quarters

We know that before dawn
One of us will be taken out and shot

We smile like conspirators
And whisper to each other
Be seeing you

We don't say when or where

We've given up the old ways
We know what we mean

Vasko Popa
(Translated by Anne Pennington)

Forced March

You're crazy. You fall down,   stand up and walk again,
your ankles and your knees move   pain that wanders around,
but you start again   as if you had wings.
The ditch calls you, but it's no use   you're afraid to stay,
and if someone asks why,   maybe you turn around and say
that a woman and a sane death   a better death wait for you.
But you're crazy.   For a long time now
only the burned wind spins   above the houses at home,
Walls lie on their backs,   plum trees are broken
and the angry night   is thick with fear.
Oh, if I could believe   that everything valuable
is not only inside me now   that there's still home to go back to.
If only there were! And just as before   bees drone peacefully
on the cool veranda,   plum preserves turn cold
and over sleepy gardens   quietly, the end of summer bathes in
    the sun.
Among the leaves the fruit   swing naked
and in front of the rust-brown hedge   blonde Fanny waits for me,
the morning writes   slow shadows –
All this could happen!   The moon is so round today!
Don't walk past me, friend.   Yell, and I'll stand up again!

September 15, 1944
Miklós Radnóti
(Translated by Steven Polgar, S. Berg & S. J. Marks)

Postcards

Nine miles from here
the haystacks and houses burn,
and on the edges of the meadow
there are quiet frightened peasants, smoking.
The little shepherd girl seems
to step into the lake, the water ripples.
The ruffled sheepfold
bends to the clouds and drinks.

Cservenka
October 6, 1944

Bloody drool hangs on the mouths of the oxen.
The men all piss red.
The company stands around in stinking wild knots.
Death blows overhead, disgusting.

Mohács
October 24, 1944

I fell next to him. His body rolled over.
It was tight as a string before it snaps.
Shot in the back of the head – 'This is how
you'll end.' 'Just lie quietly,' I said to myself.
Patience flowers into death now.
'*Der springt noch auf*,' I heard above me.
Dark filthy blood was drying on my ear.

Szentkirályszabadja
October 31, 1944

Miklós Radnóti
(Translated by Steven Polgar,
S. Berg and S. J. Marks)

Harbach 1944

At all times I see them.
The moon brilliant. A black shaft looms up.
Beneath it, harnessed men
haul an immense cart.

Dragging that giant wagon
which grows bigger as the night grows
their bodies are divided among
the dust, their hunger and their trembling.

They are carrying the road, they are carrying the land,
the bleak potato fields,
and all they know is the weight of everything,
the burden of the skylines

and the falling bodies of their companions
which almost grow into their own
as they lurch, living layers,
treading each other's footsteps.

The villages stay clear of them,
the gateways withdraw.
The distance, that has come to meet them,
reels away back.

Staggering, they wade knee deep
in the low, darkly-muffled clatter
of their wooden clogs
as through invisible leaf litter.

Already their bodies belong to silence.
And they thrust their faces towards the height
as if they strained for a scent
of the faraway celestial troughs

because, prepared for their coming
like an opened cattle-yard,
its gates flung savagely back,
death gapes to its hinges.

János Pilinszky
(Translated by Ted Hughes)

Passion of Ravensbrück

He steps out from the others.
He stands in the square silence.
The prison garb, the convict's skull
blink like a projection.

He is horribly alone.
His pores are visible.
Everything about him is so gigantic,
everything is so tiny.

And this is all.
              The rest –
the rest was simply
that he forgot to cry out
before he collapsed.

János Pilinszky
(Translated by Ted Hughes)

On the Wall of a KZ-Lager

Where you have fallen, you stay.
In the whole universe, this is your place.
Just this single spot.
But you have made this yours absolutely.

The countryside evades you.
House, mill, poplar,
each thing strives to be free of you
as if it were mutating in nothingness.

But now it is you who stay.
Did we blind you? You continue to watch us.
Did we rob you? You enriched yourself.
Speechless, speechless, you testify against us.

János Pilinszky
(Translated by Ted Hughes)

Fable

Detail from his KZ-Oratorio: Dark Heaven

Once upon a time
there was a lonely wolf
lonelier than the angels.

He happened to come to a village.
He fell in love with the first house he saw.

Already he loved its walls
the caresses of its bricklayers.
But the windows stopped him.

In the room sat people.
Apart from God nobody ever
found them so beautiful
as this child-like beast.

So at night he went into the house.
He stopped in the middle of the room
and never moved from there any more.

He stood all through the night, with wide eyes
and on into the morning when he was beaten to death.

János Pilinszky
(Translated by Ted Hughes)

Roads

Choked sunset glow
of crashing time.
Roads. Roads.
Intersections of flight.
Cart tracks across the ploughed field
that with the eyes
of killed horses
saw the sky in flames.

Nights with lungs full of smoke,
with the hard breath of the fleeing
when shots
struck the dusk.
Out of a broken gate
ash and wind came without a sound
a fire
that sullenly chewed the darkness.

Corpses,
flung over the rail tracks,
their stifled cry
like a stone on the palate.
A black
humming cloth of flies
closed over wounds.

Peter Huchel
(Translated by Michael Hamburger)

A Poem of Death

From the Rumanian of Maria Banus

And once again the angel of Death came,
this time in the guise of a baker.
He had the clothes, the face, the hands of a baker,
and all of them white with flour.
In his hand he held a shovel,
from his ovens there came the smell
of bread burned in the fire.
His movements were solemn and stately.
The wheel, the blaze and the round bread
followed each other
slowly, and for ever,
from the mouth of the furnace.

I am not afraid of you, bread-maker,
you remind me of Janus,
in the street of childhood,
the paradise of cracknel.

This was my word to him
when he raised his hidden skull towards me.
Behind him the mills of Auschwitz were grinding
and the citizen bread-maker
in his apron powdered with flour,
angel of Death, angel of fire,
spread out before my eyes
his naked wares:
hollow they all were,
covered with mushrooms
close to the roots.

George Macbeth

Night over Birkenau

Night again. Again the grim sky closes
circling like a vulture over the dead silence.
Like a crouching beast over the camp
the moon sets, pale as a corpse.

And like a shield abandoned in battle,
blue Orion – lost among the stars.
The transports growl in darkness
and the eyes of the crematorium blaze.

It's steamy, stifling. Sleep is a stone.
Breath rattles in my throat.
This lead foot crushing my chest
is the silence of three million dead.

Night, night without end. No dawn comes.
My eyes are poisoned from sleep.
Like God's judgement on the corpse of the earth,
fog descends over Birkenau.

Tadeusz Borowski
(Translated by Tadeusz Pióro)

Treblinka

A survivor speaks:

That winter night they were burning corpses
And from the bonfire, flooding the whole camp
Flared purple and blue and red and orange and gold,
The many colours of Joseph's coat, who was chosen.
Not cold for once we at the barrack windows
Blinked and listened; the opera singer,
Unafraid for once, found his full voice and gave it
To words, to a music that gushed like blood from a wound:
Eli, Eli . . . his question too in whose name
Long we'd been dirt to be wiped off, dust to be dispersed –
Older than he, old as the silence of God.
In that light we knew it; and the complaint was praise,
Was thankfulness for death, the lost and the promised land,
The gathering up at last, all our hundred hues
Fierce in one radiance gathered by greater darkness,
The darkness that took our kings, David and Solomon
Who living had burnt with the same fire;
All our hundred languages gathered again in one silence.

To live was the law; though to live – and not only here –
Was a hundred times over to spit in our own faces,
Wipe ourselves out of creation, scatter as dust,
Eat grass, and the dung that feeds grass.
The grass, the dung, the spittle – here we saw them consumed,
Even these bodies fit in the end to yield light.

Back in a room in a house in a street in a town
I forget the figures, remember little but this:
That to live is not good enough: everything, anything
Proved good enough for life – there, and not only there.
Yet we lived, a few of us, perhaps with no need but this:
To tell of the fire in the night and briefly flare like the dead.

Michael Hamburger

Shipment to Maidanek

Arrived from scattered cities, several lands,
intact from sea land, mountain land, and plain,
Item: six surgeons, slightly mangled hands,
Item: three poets, hopelessly insane,

Item: a Russian mother and her child,
the former with five gold teeth and usable shoes,
the latter with seven dresses, peasant-styled.

Item: another hundred thousand Jews.

Item: a crippled Czech with a handmade crutch.
Item: a Spaniard with a subversive laugh;
seventeen dozen Danes, nine gross of Dutch.

Total: precisely a million and a half.

They are sorted and marked – the method is up to you.
The books must be balanced, the disposition stated.
Take care that all accounts are neat and true.

Make sure that they are thoroughly cremated.

Ephraim Fogel

Remembering Dresden

(13th–15th February 1945: The British had learned a technique for placing bombs to create firestorms. The Russians were approaching Dresden.)

Dresdener:

British reconnaissance planes
Dropped flares called 'Christmas trees'
To mark the target.

At ten o'clock the first bombers
Dropped explosive bombs.
People evacuated the downtown.

Our street was filled.
At two, the firebombs caught them
Sleeping, some in tents, in the open.

St Valentine's day and the next,
American bombers pounded the ruins.

Blackened bodies shrunken to babies
Lay at the doors of churches and cellars
Or at curbs had clawed with fingernails
For shelter in the hollows of gutters.

The Frauenkirche, the Semper Galerie,
The Zwinger Museum – gutted.
A hundred major monuments smouldering.

The structure of time torn.

Forty hospitals in the eye of the firestorm.

Eight nights.
Glowing columns of smoke three miles high.
A valentine for Stalin.

Dutch Prisoner:

A nerve centre for the Reich,
Its industry made complex systems,
Its intelligence served insanity.

We went through the Florence-on-the-Elbe,
Five months before the bombing,
Past their last great

Railway-engine repair works
Working furiously. To us,
It was already the trainworks of hell.

They said we were going a bit north,
To Riesa's steelworks as slave labourers.
We were in three trains,

Sixty to a boxcar,
Fifty boxcars to a train.
Our train was repaired there.

We stayed in the cattle-cars.
They did not show us the museums.
From Dresden we went east to Auschwitz.

German Student (Evanston, Illinois,
August 1954, 2 a.m.):

It was like an oven,
The sidewalks were unbearable,
Asphalt popped in the street.

Unable to make it with both children,
She had to choose between them.
Afterwards her feet were amputated.

Van K. Brock

Passover: the Injections

Clouds pass over, endless
black fruit dripping
sap from the branches
of lightning.

We lie down in the fields,
thousands of us,
never mind the rain.

Soldiers come toward us,
groups of three or four.
The wind opens their long coats.
Underneath their uniforms are black.

They bend over the babies.
The babies cry,
for a little while.

'We are living in Biblical times,'
a woman says.

William Heyen

A Girl of Six from the Ghetto Begging in Smolna Street in 1942

she had nothing
but eyes to grow up to
in them quite by chance
two stars of David
perhaps a teardrop would put them out

so she cried

Her speech
was not silver
worth at least
a spit a turning away of the head
her tearful speech
full of hunchbacked words

so she fell silent

Her silence
was not golden
worth at most
3 ha'pence perhaps a carrot or whatever
a very well behaved silence
with a Jewish accent
of hunger

so she died

Jerzy Ficowski
(Translated by Keith Bosley)

5.8.1942
In Memory of Janusz Korczak*

What did the Old Doctor do
in the cattle wagon
bound for Treblinka on the fifth of August
over the few hours of the bloodstream
over the dirty river of time

I do not know

what did Charon of his own free will
the ferryman without an oar do
did he give out to the children
what remained of gasping breath
and leave for himself
only frost down the spine

I do not know

did he lie to them for instance
in small
numbing doses
groom the sweaty little heads
for the scurrying lice of fear

I do not know

yet for all that yet later yet there
in Treblinka
all their terror all the tears
were against him

oh it was only now
just so many minutes say a lifetime
whether a little or a lot
I was not there I do not know

suddenly the Old Doctor saw
the children had grown
as old as he was
older and older
that was how fast they had to go grey as ash

Jerzy Ficowski
(Translated by Keith Bosley)

* Janusz Korczak: 1878–1942, physician, educator, writer, born in Warsaw of assimilated Jewish family. After qualifying as a medical practitioner, he immediately turned his attention to the poor, and in particular to children, later orphans. His first publication, *Children of the Streets*, appeared in 1901. He served on the Russian front in the First World War, then headed two orphanages in Warsaw, one Jewish, one non-Jewish. He continued to write and to pioneer a more enlightened approach to the bringing up of children. At the beginning of the Second World War he was removed from the non-Jewish orphanage. He tried to ignore the Nazi occupation of Poland and refused to wear the Yellow Badge, for which he was jailed for a while. He kept a diary throughout the occupation (extant). He refused to let his Polish friends smuggle him out of the Warsaw Ghetto to the 'Aryan side' as he was not prepared to leave his orphans to face their fate alone.

On 5th August, 1942, (title of Ficowski's poem), the Germans rounded up Dr Korczak, his staff, and his 200 children and marched them three miles to the deportation train. An eyewitness reported to Emanuel Ringelblum, who kept daily records of life in the Ghetto, that Korczak ordered his orphans to march in a disciplined way with their heads held high and looking at no one. He led them, and his staff, holding a child's hand in each of his. On arrival at Treblinka they were all gassed to death.

from Holocaust

Once, among the transports, was one with children – two
   freight cars full.
The young men sorting out the belongings of those taken to
   the gas chambers
had to undress the children – they were orphans –
and then take them to the 'lazarette.'
There the SS men shot them.

A large eight-wheeled car arrived at the hospital
where there were children;
in the two trailers – open trucks – were sick women and men
lying on the floor.
The Germans threw the children into the trucks
from the second floor and the balconies –
children from one year old to ten;
threw them upon the sick in the trucks.
Some of the children tried to hold on to the walls,
scratched at the walls with their nails;
but the shouting Germans
beat and pushed the children towards the windows.

The children arrived at the camp in buses,
guarded by gendarmes of the French Vichy government.
The buses stopped in the middle of the courtyard
and the children were quickly taken off
to make room for the buses following.
Frightened but quiet,
the children came down in groups of fifty or sixty to eighty;
the younger children holding on to older ones.
They were taken upstairs to empty halls –
without any furniture
and only dirty straw bags on the floor, full of bugs:
children as young as two, three, or four years of age,
all in torn clothes and dirty,

for they had already spent two or three weeks in other camps,
uncared for
and were now on their way to a death camp in Poland.
Some had only one shoe.
Many had diarrhoea
but they were not allowed in the courtyard
where the water-closets were;
and, although there were chamber pots in the corridor of each
     story,
these were too large for the small children.

The women in the camp who were also deportees
and about to be taken to other camps
were in tears:
they would get up before sunrise
and go into the halls where the children were –
in each a hundred to a hundred and twenty –
to mend the children's clothing;
but the women had no soap to clean the children,
no clean underwear to give them,
and only cold water with which to wash them.
When soup came for the children,
there were no spoons;
and it would be served in tins
but the tins were sometimes too hot for the children to hold.

A visitor once stopped one of the children:
a boy of seven or eight, handsome, alert and gay.
He had only one shoe and the other foot was bare,
and his coat of good quality had no buttons.
The visitor asked him for his name
and then what his parents were doing;
and he said, 'Father is working in the office
and Mother is playing the piano.'
Then he asked the visitor if he would be joining his parents
    soon –
they always told the children they would be leaving soon to
    rejoin their parents –
and the visitor answered, 'Certainly. In a day or two.'
At that the child took out of his pocket
half an army biscuit he had been given in camp
and said, 'I am keeping this half for Mother';
and then the child who had been so gay
burst into tears.

Charles Reznikoff

A Dead Child Speaks

My mother held me by my hand.
Then someone raised the knife of parting:
So that it should not strike me,
My mother loosed her hand from mine.
But she lightly touched my thighs once more
And her hand was bleeding –

After that the knife of parting
Cut in two each bite I swallowed –
It rose before me with the sun at dawn
And began to sharpen itself in my eyes –
Wind and water ground in my ear
And every voice of comfort pierced my heart –

As I was led to death
I still felt in the last moment
The unsheathing of the great knife of parting.

Nelly Sachs
(Translated by Ruth & Matthew Mead)

Already Embraced by the Arm of Heavenly Solace

Already embraced by the arm of heavenly solace
The insane mother stands
With the tatters of her torn mind
With the charred tinders of her burnt mind
Burying her dead child,
Burying her lost light,
Twisting her hands into urns,
Filling them with the body of her child from the air,
Filling them with his eyes, his hair from the air,
And with his fluttering heart –

Then she kisses the air-born being
And dies!

Nelly Sachs
(Translated by Michael Roloff)

O the Night of the Weeping Children!

O the night of the weeping children!
O the night of the children branded for death!
Sleep may not enter here.
Terrible nursemaids
Have usurped the place of mothers,
Have tautened their tendons with the false death,
Sown it on to the walls and into the beams –
Everywhere it is hatched in the nests of horror.
Instead of mother's milk, panic suckles those little ones.

Yesterday Mother still drew
Sleep toward them like a white moon,
There was the doll with cheeks derouged by kisses
In one arm,
The stuffed pet, already
Brought to life by love,
In the other –
Now blows the wind of dying,
Blows the shifts over the hair
That no one will comb again.

Nelly Sachs
(Translated by Michael Hamburger)

Massacre of the Boys

The children cried 'Mummy!
But I have been good!
It's dark in here! Dark!'

See them They are going to the bottom
See the small feet
they went to the bottom Do you see
that print
of a small foot here and there

pockets bulging
with string and stones
and little horses made of wire

A great closed plain
like a figure of geometry
and a tree of black smoke
a vertical
dead tree
with no star in its crown.

The Museum, Auschwitz, 1948

Tadeusz Różewicz
(Translated by Adam Czerniawski)

Pigtail

When all the women in the transport
had their heads shaved
four workmen with brooms made of birch
    twigs
swept up
and gathered up the hair

Behind clean glass
the stiff hair lies
of those suffocated in gas chambers
there are pins and side combs
in this hair

The hair is not shot through with light
is not parted by the breeze
is not touched by any hand
or rain or lips

In huge chests
clouds of dry hair
of those suffocated
and a faded plait
a pigtail with a ribbon
pulled at school
by naughty boys.

The Museum, Auschwitz, 1948

Tadeusz Różewicz
(Translated by Adam Czerniawski)

In the Camp There Was One Alive

(This is a concentration camp burned by its guards,
deserted by its prisoners, and not yet occupied by the Allies.)

Flakes pour to the black dead
At Lasen, by the wire.
The child, in his charred cave,
Watches the shaking fire

Struggle to him in torment
Till, stumbling, the shades sink back
Into his helplessness; his shaking
Limbs shrink to nothing, crack

Under the beams that pin him.
He hears, beneath the hiss
Of snow, a step on snow, the vague
Murmur of many voices.

They have come; and he calls to them
In gladness – it is the dead.
They speak softly, he understands
Nothing, and inches his head

Back over to them; but he sees
Nothing, he hears nothing. He moans
In his last loneliness – and the voices
Ring in his ears, the stones

Are flung from the hammering feet
Of the dead who cry
The child's name over and over.
He laughs out in joy

And wrenches with all his strength
Against the timbers, cries:
'I'm coming.' The voices are fainter,
The footsteps die as he dies.

Randall Jarrell

Magda Goebbels

30 April 1945

*(After Dr Haase gave them shots of
morphine, Magda gave each child an
ampoule of potassium cyanide from a
spoon.)*

This is the needle that we give
Soldiers and children when they live
Near the front in primitive
    Conditions or real dangers;
This is the spoon we use to feed
Men trapped in trouble or in need,
When weakness or bad luck might lead
    Them to the hands of strangers.

This is the room where you can sleep
Your sleep out, curled up under deep
Layers of covering that will keep
    You safe till all harm's past.
This is the bed where you can rest
In perfect silence, undistressed
By noise or nightmares, as my breast
    Once held you soft but fast.

• • •

This is the glass tube that contains
Calm that will spread down through your veins
To free you finally from all pains
    Of going on in error.
This tiny pinprick sets the germ
Inside you that fills out its term
Till you can feel yourself grow firm
    Against all doubt, all terror.

Into this spoon I break the pill
That stiffens the unsteady will
And hardens you against the chill
   Voice of a world of lies.
This amber medicine implants
Steadfastness in your blood; this grants
Immunity from greed and chance,
   And from all compromise.

• • •

I set this spoon between your tight
Teeth, as I gave you your first bite;
This satisfies your appetite
   For other nourishment.
Take this on your tongue; this do
Remembering your mother who
So loved her Leader she stayed true
   When all the others went,

When every friend proved false, in the
Delirium of treachery
On every hand, when even He
   Had turned His face aside.
He shut himself in with His whore;
Then, though I screamed outside His door,
Said He'd not see me any more.
   They both took cyanide.

Open wide, now, little bird;
I who sang you your first word
Soothe away every sound you've heard
   Except your Leader's voice.
Close your eyes, now; take your death.
Once we slapped you to take breath.
Vengeance is mine, the Lord God saith
   And cancels each last choice.

W. D. Snodgrass

Burnt

Burdened with family feelings, I went
To my aunt's place,
           to see my uncle,

To press my girl cousins to my breast,
Who were so carried away,
              as it happened,
By music and the other arts!

I found neither uncle nor aunt,
I did not see my cousins either,
But I remember,
          remember
              to this day,
How their neighbours,
            looking down at the ground,
Said to me quietly: They were burnt.

Everything's gone up in flames: the vices with the virtues,
And children with their aged parents.
And there am I, standing before these hushed witnesses,
And quietly repeating:
           burnt.

Boris Slutsky
(Translated by Daniel Weissbort)

Innocence

(*to Tony White*)

He ran the course and as he ran he grew,
And smelt his fragrance in the field. Already,
Running he knew the most he ever knew,
The egotism of a healthy body.

Ran into manhood, ignorant of the past:
Culture of guilt and guilt's vague heritage,
Self-pity and the soul; what he possessed
Was rich, potential, like the bud's tipped rage.

The Corps developed, it was plain to see,
Courage, endurance, loyalty and skill
To a morale firm as morality,
Hardening him to an instrument, until

The finitude of virtues that were there
Bodied within the swarthy uniform
A compact innocence, child-like and clear,
No doubt could penetrate, no act could harm.

When he stood near the Russian partisan
Being burned alive, he therefore could behold
The ribs wear gently through the darkening skin
And sicken only at the Northern cold,

Could watch the fat burn with a violet flame
And feel disgusted only at the smell,
And judge that all pain finishes the same
As melting quietly by his boots it fell.

Thom Gunn

from Holocaust

Jews from Holland, France, and Hungary, and later from
    Greece,
were brought to a camp in freight trains or cattle cars –
three or four trains a day –
the cars crowded
and on the road days and nights,
with nothing for those inside
to eat or drink;
and when the cars were at the camp
they were driven out with whips
and blows from the butts of rifles.
They were then lined up before the camp physician
and as they passed before him
he would ask their age of the men – if they did not show it –
and what they did for a living,
and then point with his thumb
to the right or left;
and those sent to the left – all able to work –
were driven barefoot to the camp,
even when snow was on the ground,
and whipped to go faster.
One of the soldiers on guard said as a joke,
pointing to the smoke from the chimneys of the crematorium,
'The only road from here to freedom!'

Some of those sent to the right
would be loaded on vans
with only a single member of an SS squad
seated in front
and were gassed in the van –
if it was that kind –
and their bodies brought straight to the crematorium.
But most would be brought to the gas chambers
behind trees that had been cut down
and set up in rows.

If the gas chambers were crowded
and no room for the youngest children – or even adults –
they were thrown on piles of wood
that had been sprinkled with gasoline
and just burnt alive.
But that their screams might not be too disturbing
to those who worked
an orchestra of Jews from the camp
was set to playing loudly
well-known German songs.

· · ·

A woman came with her little daughter
and SS men were there one morning
and took the child away:
a mother was forbidden to keep her child with her.
Later, the woman found out that her child had been thrown
    into the fire
in which the dead were being burnt,
and that night threw herself against the electrified barbed wire
    fence around the camp.

· · ·

In the morning the Jews were lined up by an officer
and the officer told them:
'You are Jews, unworthy of life,
but are now supposed to work.'
They were put upon trucks
and taken away to a forest
and set to digging.
After two or three spadefuls of earth,
the spade of one hit something hard,
and he saw that it was the head of a human being.
There was also a bad smell all around.
He stopped digging
and the officer in charge came towards him shouting:
'Why did you stop?
Didn't you know there are bodies buried here?'
He had opened a mass grave.

There were about ten thousand dead in that grave.
And after they had dug up the bodies
they were told to burn them.
Planks had been brought and beams – long and heavy.
The Germans also brought a grinding machine to grind the
    bones
and the ground bones would be sieved
for the gold fillings of teeth.
The dust of the bones would then be spread over the fields,
and the smell was dreadful.

They kept on working three months
opening mass graves;
and opened eight or nine.
In one those digging saw a boy of two or three,
lying on his mother's body.
He had little white shoes on
and a little white jacket,
and his face was pressed against his mother's.

One grave would remain open for new corpses
coming all the time;
a truck would bring the bodies, still warm,
to be thrown into the grave –
naked as Adam and Eve;
Jewish men, many of them bearded, and Jewish women and
    children.
The graves they had opened would be refilled with earth
and they had to plant grass all over them;
as for the dead –
a thousand bodies would be put on a pyre;
and there were two pyres of bodies burning all the time.

Charles Reznikoff

Rescuers, Bystanders, Perpetrators

Both Your Mothers

for Bieta

Under a futile Torah
under an imprisoned star
your mother gave birth to you

you have proof of her
beyond doubt and death
the scar of the navel
the sign of parting for ever
which had no time to hurt you

this you know

Later you slept in a bundle
carried out of the ghetto
someone said in a chest
knocked together somewhere in Nowolipie Street
with a hole to let in air
but not fear
hidden in a cartload of bricks

You slipped out in this little coffin
redeemed by stealth
from that world to this world
all the way to the Aryan side
and fire took over
the corner you left vacant

So you did not cry
crying could have meant death
luminal hummed you
its lullaby
And you nearly were not
so that you could be

But the mother
who was saved in you
could now step into crowded death
happily incomplete
could instead of memory give you
for a parting gift
her own likeness
and a date and a name

so much

And at once a chance
someone hastily
bustled about your sleep
and then stayed for a long always
and washed you of orphanhood
and swaddled you in love
and become the answer
to your first word

That was how
both your mothers taught you
not to be surprised at all
when you say
I am

Jerzy Ficowski
(Translated by Keith Bosley)

1980

And when I go up as a pilgrim in winter, to recover
the place I was born, and the twin to self I am in my mind,
then I'll go in black snow as a pilgrim to find
the grave of my saviour, Yanova.

She'll hear what I whisper, under my breath:
Thank you. You saved my tears from the flame.
Thank you. Children and grandchildren you rescued from
    death.
I planted a sapling (it doesn't suffice) in your name.

Time in its gyre spins back down the flue
faster than nightmares of nooses can ride,
quicker than nails. And you, my saviour, in your cellar you'll
    hide
me, ascending in dreams as a pilgrim to you.

You'll come from the yard in your slippers, crunching the
    snow
so I'll know. Again I'm there in the cellar, degraded and low,
you're bringing me milk and bread sliced thick at the edge.
You're making the sign of the cross. I'm making my pencil its
    pledge.

Abraham Sutzkever
(Translated by Cynthia Ozick)

I Did Not Manage To Save

I did not manage to save
a single life

I did not know how to stop
a single bullet

and I wander round cemeteries
which are not there

I look for words
which are not there
I run

to help where no one called
to rescue after the event

I want to be on time
even if I am too late

Jerzy Ficowski
(Translated by Keith Bosley &
Krystyna Wandycz)

A Poor Christian Looks at the Ghetto

Bees build around red liver,
Ants build around black bone.
It has begun: the tearing, the trampling on silks,
It has begun: the breaking of glass, wood, copper, nickel, silver,
    foam
Of gypsum, iron sheets, violin strings, trumpets, leaves, balls,
    crystals.
Poof! Phosphorescent fire from yellow walls
Engulfs animal and human hair.

Bees build around the honeycomb of lungs,
Ants build around white bone.
Torn is paper, rubber, linen, leather, flax,
Fibre, fabrics, cellulose, snakeskin, wire.
The roof and the wall collapse in flame and heat seizes the
    foundations.
Now there is only the earth, sandy, trodden down,
With one leafless tree.

Slowly, boring a tunnel, a guardian mole makes his way,
With a small red lamp fastened to his forehead.
He touches buried bodies, counts them, pushes on,
He distinguishes human ashes by their luminous vapour,
The ashes of each man by a different part of the spectrum.
Bees build around a red trace.
Ants build around the place left by my body.

I am afraid, so afraid of the guardian mole.
He has swollen eyelids, like a Patriarch
Who has sat much in the light of candles
Reading the great book of the species.

What will I tell him, I, a Jew of the New Testament,
Waiting two thousand years for the second coming of Jesus?
My broken body will deliver me to his sight
And he will count me among the helpers of death:
The uncircumcised.

Warsaw, 1943*   *Czeslaw Milosz*

* After the Jewish uprising, the Warsaw Ghetto was destroyed on 15th May, 1943. The German officer commanding, Brigadier Stroop, proudly informed Berlin, 'The Warsaw Ghetto is no more.'

History and Reality

'Sin is nothing but the refusal to recognize human misery.'
SIMONE WEIL

I
Escaped from Germany –
Cared for by English friends, with whom
Kindness counted still –

Rumours reached her –

Photographs made by the Gestapo –

Jews, her people –
So various, all one –

Each taken full-face –

The strong – the meek – the sad – the proud.

Hunger had stretched the parchment skin
Across the contours of the bone –
Forehead, cheek-bones, chin.

And in each face there was the same
Ultimate revelation
Of eyes that stare upon the real –

Some terrible final thing.

II

She locked herself inside her room,
Her mind filled with those images
From Germany, her homeland, where
Those deaths were the reality –

Real! – not some tragedy that actors
Performed before an audience –
Pity and terror purifying
The onlooker, enraptured by
Poetry secreted in the lines.
But where the players were the victims
Massacred from a tyrant's mouth.

She felt a kind of envy for
Those who stood naked in their truth:
Where to be one of her people was
To be one of those millions killed.

III

She starved her body to pure thought
To be one with her people snatched
From ghettos by the SS, then
Hurled into cattle trucks of trains
Hurtling all night across bare plains
Till dawn, when there stood, waiting on
Platforms of sidings (below walls
Of concrete and barbed wire) – guards, who
Marched them to a parade-ground, where
Those fit to work in factories
Were separated from the rest –
Women and children, the old, the sick,

Who taken to a yard, were robbed
Of jewellery, satchels, playthings, shoes –
Things that to them meant home and name –
And made to stand there when a voice
From a watch-tower proclaimed they would
Be cleansed of lice, and being Jews.

IV
Then thrust inside a shed where she
Through her intense imagining
Stood there among them bodily
When, from outside, the guards turned on
Taps through which hissed not water but
The murdering gas, whereon that crowd
Breathed a great sigh of revelation –
Their life, their death – for her the real
Instant where history ground its wheel
On her with them, inside that moment
When – outside – truth was only words.

Stephen Spender

Babii Yar*

No monument stands over Babii Yar.
A drop sheer as a crude gravestone.
I am afraid.

        Today I am as old in years
as all the Jewish people.
Now I seem to be

        a Jew.
Here I plod through ancient Egypt.
Here I perish crucified, on the cross,
and to this day I bear the scars of nails.
I seem to be

        Dreyfus.
The Philistine

        is both informer and judge.
I am behind bars.

        Beset on every side.
Hounded,

      spat on,

        slandered.

Squealing, dainty ladies in flounced Brussels lace
stick their parasols into my face.
I seem to be then

        a young boy in Byelostok.
Blood runs, spilling over the floors.
The barroom rabble-rousers
give off a stench of vodka and onion.
A boot kicks me aside, helpless.
In vain I plead with these pogrom bullies.
While they jeer and shout,

        'Beat the Yids. Save Russia!'

* One of five Yevtushenko poems on which Dmitri Shostakovich based his
Thirteenth Symphony. Babii Yar: Ravine in the suburbs of Kiev where Nazi
forces murdered 33,000 Soviet Jews. For a long time there was no monument
at the site of the atrocity.

Some grain-marketeer beats up my mother.
O my Russian people!
                              I know
                                         you
are international to the core.
But those with unclean hands
have often made a jingle of your purest name.
I know the goodness of my land.
How vile these anti-Semites –
                                             without a qualm
they pompously called themselves
the Union of the Russian People!

I seem to be
                    Anne Frank
transparent
                    as a branch in April.
And I love.
                    And have no need of phrases.
My need
           is that we gaze into each other.
How little we can see
                              or smell!
We are denied the leaves,
                                   we are denied the sky.
Yet we can do so much –
                                   tenderly
embrace each other in a darkened room.
They're coming here?
                              Be not afraid. Those are the booming
sounds of spring:
                         spring is coming here.
Come then to me.
                         Quick, give me your lips.
Are they smashing down the door?
                                             No, it's the ice breaking. . .
The wild grasses rustle over Babii Yar.

The trees look ominous,
                    like judges.
Here all things scream silently,
                        and, baring my head,
slowly I feel myself
                turning grey.
And I myself
            am one massive, soundless scream
above the thousand thousand buried here.
I am
      each old man
                here shot dead.
I am
      every child
                here shot dead.
Nothing in me
            shall ever forget!
The 'Internationale,' let it
                        thunder
when the last anti-Semite on earth
is buried for ever.
In my blood there is no Jewish blood.
In their callous rage, all anti-Semites
must hate me now as a Jew.
For that reason
            I am a true Russian!

Yevgeny Yevtushenko
(Translated by George Reavey)

Ovid in the Third Reich

non peccat, quaecumque potest peccasse negare,
*solaque famosam culpa professa facit.**
                              (Amores, III: xiv)

I love my work and my children. God
Is distant, difficult. Things happen.
Too near the ancient troughs of blood
Innocence is no earthly weapon.

I have learned one thing: not to look down
So much upon the damned. They, in their sphere,
Harmonize strangely with the divine
Love. I, in mine, celebrate the love-choir.

Geoffrey Hill

* She does not sin who can deny her sin,
'Tis only the fault avowed that brings dishonour.

September Song

born 19.6.32 – deported 24.9.42

Undesirable you may have been, untouchable
you were not. Not forgotten
or passed over at the proper time.

As estimated, you died. Things marched,
sufficient, to that end.
Just so much Zyklon and leather, patented
terror, so many routine cries.

(I have made
an elegy for myself it
is true)

September fattens on vines. Roses
flake from the wall. The smoke
of harmless fires drifts to my eyes.

This is plenty. This is more than enough.

Geoffrey Hill

A Camp in the Prussian Forest

I walk beside the prisoners to the road.
Load on puffed load,
Their corpses, stacked like sodden wood,
Lie barred or galled with blood

By the charred warehouse. No one comes today
In the old way
To knock the fillings from their teeth;
The dark, coned, common wreath

Is plaited for their grave – a kind of grief.
The living leaf
Clings to the planted profitable
Pine if it is able;

The boughs sigh, mile on green, calm, breathing mile,
From this dead file
The planners ruled for them. . .One year
They sent a million here:

Here men were drunk like water, burnt like wood.
The fat of good
And evil, the breast's star of hope
Were rendered into soap.

I paint the star I sawed from yellow pine –
And plant the sign
In soil that does not yet refuse
Its usual Jews

Their first asylum. But the white, dwarfed star –
This dead white star –
Hides nothing, pays for nothing; smoke
Fouls it, a yellow joke,

The needles of the wreath are chalked with ash,
A filmy trash
Litters the black woods with the death
Of men; and one last breath

Curls from the monstrous chimney . . . I laugh aloud
Again and again;
The star laughs from its rotting shroud
Of flesh. O star of men!

Randall Jarrell

'More Light! More Light!'

for Heinrich Blücher and Hannah Arendt

Composed in the Tower before his execution
These moving verses, and being brought at that time
Painfully to the stake, submitted, declaring thus:
'I implore my God to witness that I have made no crime.'

Nor was he forsaken of courage, but the death was horrible,
The sack of gunpowder failing to ignite.
His legs were blistered sticks on which the black sap
Bubbles and burst as he howled for the Kindly Light.

And that was but one, and by no means one of the worst;
Permitted at least his pitiful dignity;
And such as were by made prayers in the name of Christ,
That shall judge all men, for his soul's tranquillity.

We move now to outside a German wood.
Three men are there commanded to dig a hole
In which the two Jews are ordered to lie down
And be buried alive by the third, who is a Pole.

Not light from the shrine at Weimar beyond the hill
Nor light from heaven appeared. But he did refuse.
A Luger settled back deeply in its glove.
He was ordered to change places with the Jews.

Much casual death had drained away their souls.
The thick dirt mounted toward the quivering chin.
When only the head was exposed the order came
To dig him out again and to get back in.

No light, no light in the blue Polish eye.
When he finished a riding boot packed down the earth.
The Luger hovered lightly in its glove.
He was shot in the belly and in three hours bled to death.

No prayers or incense rose up in those hours
Which grew to be years, and every day came mute
Ghosts from the ovens, sifting through crisp air,
And settled upon his eyes in a black soot.

Anthony Hecht

Between the Lines

Yesterday, just before being transported
back to prison, I committed a terrible
gaffe. Two people came out of the interrogation
room. One of them, tall, elegant,
speaking a very cultivated French, looked
so tormented, as though about to break
down. I asked him with concern: 'Vous
ont-ils malmené?' 'Qui ça?' 'Mais eux.'
He looked at me, shrugged his shoulders
and walked on. Then the Germany sentry said:
'But that's a Gestapo man.'

                Prison Diary of E. A. Rheinhardt,
                        Nice, Jan. 22nd 1944.

Later, back in my cell, back in the thick stench
From the bucket shared with three men whose dreams
    are of flesh
Not for beating or fondling but eating, I laugh, laugh
As never before in that place, even when gorged with a treat
Of gift food from a parcel. For then I would drift
Away from our common attrition by hunger and filth
To my garden, those hardly believable flowers
That may open again though I am not there to tend them,
To my bed and, almost, the mingling of bodies in lust,
And would hate the voice that clattered into my refuge
With a curse or a joke. Now they are close to me,
My fellow victims, decent men at the most,
Blundering into death as I do, devoid of a fury to hurl
Against our tormentors, the furious burners of books
Numb with the icy need to know nothing, be strong.

* 'Did they treat you badly?' 'Whom d'you mean?' 'But they [the Gestapo] of
course.'

I laugh, laugh at their strength, at our feebleness
And laughing feel how one I could not believe in
Allows me to blaze like his martyrs, consumes me
With love, with compassion; and how the soul
Anatomists cannot locate even now will rise up
When my turn comes to blunder again, when I cry
To the killer who cracks my joints: 'Je te comprends,
  mon ami . . .'

Michael Hamburger

A German Requiem

It is not what they built. It is what they knocked down.
It is not the houses. It is the spaces between the houses.
It is not the streets that exist. It is the streets that no longer
    exist.
It is not your memories which haunt you.
It is not what you have written down.
It is what you have forgotten, what you must forget.
What you must go on forgetting all your life.
And with any luck oblivion should discover a ritual.
You will find out that you are not alone in the enterprise.
Yesterday the very furniture seemed to reproach you.
Today you take your place in the Widow's Shuttle.

The bus is waiting at the southern gate
To take you to the city of your ancestors
Which stands on the hill opposite, with gleaming pediments,
As vivid as this charming square, your home.
Are you shy? You should be. It is almost like a wedding,
The way you clasp your flowers and give a little tug at your
    veil. Oh,
The hideous bridesmaids, it is natural that you should resent
    them
Just a little, on this first day.
But that will pass, and the cemetery is not far.
Here comes the driver, flicking a toothpick into the gutter,
His tongue still searching between his teeth.
See, he has not noticed you. No one has noticed you.
It will pass, young lady, it will pass.

How comforting it is, once or twice a year,
To get together and forget the old times.
As on those special days, ladies and gentlemen,
When the boiled shirts gather at the graveside
And a leering waistcoat approaches the rostrum.
It is like a solemn pact between the survivors.
The mayor has signed it on behalf of the freemasonry.
The priest has sealed it on behalf of all the rest.
Nothing more need be said, and it is better that way –

The better for the widow, that she should not live in fear of
    surprise,
The better for the young man, that he should move at liberty
    between the armchairs,
The better that these bent figures who flutter among the
    graves
Tending the nightlights and replacing the chrysanthemums
Are not ghosts,
That they shall go home.
The bus is waiting, and on the upper terraces
The workmen are dismantling the houses of the dead.

But when so many had died, so many and at such speed,
There were no cities waiting for the victims.
They unscrewed the nameplates from the shattered doorways
And carried them away with the coffins.
So the squares and parks were filled with the eloquence of
    young cemeteries:
The smell of fresh earth, the improvised crosses
And all the impossible directions in brass and enamel.

'Doctor Gliedschirm, skin specialist, surgeries 14–16 hours or
    by appointment.'
Professor Sargnagel was buried with four degrees, two
    associate memberships
And instructions to tradesmen to use the back entrance.
Your uncle's grave informed you that he lived on the third
    floor, left.
You were asked please to ring, and he would come down in
    the lift
To which one needed a key . . .

Would come down, would ever come down
With a smile like thin gruel, and never too much to say.
How he shrank through the years.
How you towered over him in the narrow cage,
How he shrinks now. . .

But come. Grief must have its term? Guilt too, then.
And it seems there is no limit to the resourcefulness of
    recollection.
So that a man might say and think:
When the world was at its darkest,
When the black wings passed over the rooftops
(And who can divine His purposes?) even then
There was always, always a fire in this hearth.
You see this cupboard? A priest-hole!
And in that lumber-room whole generations have been
    housed and fed.
Oh, if I were to begin, if I were to begin to tell you
The half, the quarter, a mere smattering of what we went
    through!

His wife nods, and a secret smile,
Like a breeze with enough strength to carry one dry leaf
Over two pavingstones, passes from chair to chair.
Even the enquirer is charmed.
He forgets to pursue the point.
It is not what he wants to know.
It is what he wants not to know.
It is not what they say.
It is what they do not say.

James Fenton

Afterwards

Archive Film Material

At first it seemed a swaying field of flowers
wind blown beside a railway track, but then
I saw it was the turning heads of men
unloaded from the cattle trucks at Auschwitz.

Ruth Fainlight

Far, Far a City Lies
from 'My Little Sister'

Far, far
A city lies. Body still warm.
Bells ringing.

You have not seen a city thrust on its
    back like a horse in its blood, jerking
    its hooves unable to rise.

Bells are ringing.
City.
City.
How mourn a city whose people
    are dead and whose dead are alive in the heart.

Bells.

• • •

To watch with soft eyes
the rising morning. Wipe from the lips
the taste of hot ash.
To bring back
a world to innocence,
as if to its socket a bone
from the foot of the dead.
To return there!
To the city,

and plant there again chestnut trees
in the square,
common bellflowers
near the fence,
and not to fear,
not to fear that the beating darkness
will suddenly close up your sobs
in the bars of a song.

Fragile, my sister!
My fragile sister.

•   •   •

In seventy-seven funerals we circled the wall
and the wall stood.
From the promised land I called you,
I looked for you
among heaps of small shoes.
At every approaching holiday.

No man will cure,
nor heaven,
the offence of your scalding silence.

My blessing
did not light your eyes.
My curse
came too late.

– to say goodbye to you
even in one word
whispered

that you were no burden to us.
On the way.
Mother walked heavy.

•   •   •

We knew what the hazards were –
to cross the soft earth,
to pass by the glowing iron
and to say to a stranger
– a world was here.

It comes upon me from behind
– a choir of stones
here!
In the unrepenting street of the city
the shorn head of my sister
breaks out of a wall.

•   •   •

All your brothers.
And the desperate convoy.
Our strength did not give out,
only the earth below gave out.

No entry to sheds.
On cold stoves.
When we made our beds on steaming
dung.
Before eyes wet
with rotten joy.
In the face of dogs
too proud to bark –

even when shame came into all my limbs,
with transparent nails glaring,
we clung to our flesh
as if alive.

Until we lay down our heads
one near the other.
Until we saw our faces
one within the other.
At the edge of the redeeming pit,
my sister,
we remembered your going alone.

You were not privileged to be condemned to death.
You did not enter a covenant of blood.
On the day when you will be spoken for –
behold you
are consecrated*
more than eagles
and angels.

Abba Kovner
(Translated by Shirley Kaufman)

---

* *Behold you are consecrated*: Part of the formula recited by the groom to the
bride during the marriage ceremony: 'Behold you are consecrated unto me
with this ring according to the law of Moses and Israel.' The previous line
also alluded to a wedding, being a verbatim quotation from Song of Songs
viii, 8, the verse that introduces the little sister who is to be married.

Auschwitz, 1987

and nobody shouts halt,
and nobody fires,
and yet this deathly
silence fills one's ears

and no one slaps your face,
or whips your back, your eyes,
and no one weeps,
nor do the skies cry out

even though we have arrived
at this well known place
with its resonant name:
Auschwitz.

Adam Zych
(Translated by Hilda Schiff)

Memento

Remember the blackness of that flesh
Tarring the bones with a thin varnish
Belsen Theresienstadt Buchenwald where
Faces were a clenched despair
Knocking at the bird-song-fretted air.

Their eyes sunk jellied in their holes
Were held up to the sun like begging bowls
Their hands like rakes with finger-nails of rust
Scratched for a little kindness from the dust.
To many, in its beak, no dove brought answer.

Stephen Spender

Leave Us

Forget us
forget our generation
live like humans
forget us

we envied
plants and stones
we envied dogs

I'd rather be a rat
I told her then

I'd rather not be
I'd rather sleep
and wake when war is over
she said her eyes shut

Forget us
don't enquire about our youth
leave us

Tadeusz Różewicz
(Translated by Adam Czerniawski)

Reveille

In the brutal nights we used to dream
Dense violent dreams,
Dreamed with soul and body:
To return; to eat; to tell the story.
Until the dawn command
Sounded brief, low:
  'Wstawać':
And the heart cracked in the breast.

Now we have found our homes again,
Our bellies are full,
We're through telling the story.
It's time. Soon we'll hear again
The strange command:
  'Wstawać'.

11 January 1946   *Primo Levi*
  (Translated by Ruth Feldman & Brian Swann)

The Survivor

to B. V.

Dopo di allora, ad ora incerta,
Since then, at an uncertain hour,
That agony returns:
And till my ghastly tale is told,
This heart within me burns.

Once more he sees his companions' faces
Livid in the first faint light,
Grey with cement dust,
Nebulous in the mist,
Tinged with death in their uneasy sleep.
At night, under the heavy burden
Of their dreams, their jaws move,
Chewing a nonexistent turnip.
'Stand back, leave me alone, submerged people,
Go away. I haven't dispossessed anyone,
Haven't usurped anyone's bread.
No one died in my place. No one.
Go back into your mist.
It's not my fault if I live and breathe,
Eat, drink, sleep and put on clothes.'

4 February 1984   *Primo Levi*
             (Translated by Ruth Feldman & Brian Swann)

The Sun of Auschwitz

You remember the sun of Auschwitz
and the green of the distant meadows, lightly
lifted to the clouds by birds,
no longer green in the clouds,
but seagreen white. Together
we stood looking into the distance and felt
the far away green of the meadows and the clouds'
seagreen white within us,
as if the colour of the distant meadows
were our blood or the pulse
beating within us, as if the world
existed only through us and nothing changed
as long as we were there. I remember
your smile as elusive
as a shade of the colour of the wind,
a leaf trembling on the edge
of sun and shadow, fleeting
yet always there. So you are
for me today, in the seagreen
sky, the greenery and
the leaf-rustling wind. I feel
you in every shadow, every movement,
and you put the world around me
like your arms. I feel the world
as your body, you look into my eyes
and call me with the whole world.

Tadeusz Borowski
(Translated by Tadeusz Pióro)

Farewell to Maria

If you are living, remember
I'm alive. But don't come to me.
In this black, swollen night
snowflakes cling to the windows

And the wind whistles. And naked shapes
of trees slap the window. And above me
like smoke from charred cities and battle fronts
drifts the deaf, measureless silence.

This appalling silence! Why have I
lived so long? Now, only bitterness.
Don't come back to me. My love
burned away in the flames of the crematorium.

There, you were mine. Your body
covered in scabies and boils, rose up
like a cloud. There you were mine,
from heaven, from fire. Now it's over.

You won't come back to me. Nor will
that wind return, drunk with fog.
The dead will not rise from common graves
and brittle ash won't come back to life.

I don't want it, don't come back. It was all
playacting, a fiction, hollow theatrics.
Your love circles above me
like human smoke above the wind.

Tadeusz Borowski
(Translated by Tadeusz Pióro)

The Execution of Memory

When the first patches of snow
melt
on the mudbanks
by the little town
spats splash

a black procession
of grey-bearded
hassidim returns

they recognize old Abie

rooks
harshly enunciate
Hebrew verses
of twigs

Here once a synagogue stood
with a bird-belfry of poplars

Boughs lifted
like hands
greet the salvo of silence

and memory killed
falls
a leafless skeleton of shadow
headlong

and the sudden passing of time
with the thaw bleeds again
          ~
I would like just to be silent
but being silent I lie

I would like just to walk
but walking I trample

Jerzy Ficowski
(Translated by Keith Bosley)

My Mother's Friend

My mother
had a schoolfriend
she shared the war with

my mother
looked after her friend
in the ghetto

she laid her out
as though she was dead
and the Gestapo overlooked her

in Auschwitz
she fed her friend snow
when she was burning with typhoid

and when
the Nazis
emptied Stuthof

they threw
the inmates
onto boats in the Baltic

and tried
to drown
as many as they could

my mother
and her friend
survived

in
Bayreuth
after the war

my mother's friend
patted my cheeks
and curled my curls

and hurled herself
from the top
of a bank.

Lily Brett

La Pathétique

I put on La Pathétique
the sound invades my skin
enlarges my heart

the notes drop
into channels
of sadness

piercing
puncturing
pain

Beethoven
must have been
brokenhearted
when he wrote this sonata

I hum
I nod my head
I conduct the performance
from my car

this listening
to music
is new to me

for years
I required silence

I was listening
for murderers

I was expecting
menace

I was prepared
for peril

I was waiting
for disaster

and
couldn't be disturbed.

Lily Brett

I, the Survivor

I know of course; it's simply luck
That I've survived so many friends. But last night in a dream
I heard those friends say of me: 'Survival of the fittest'
And I hated myself.

Bertolt Brecht
(Translated by John Willet)

The Return

Suddenly the window will open
and Mother will call
it's time to come in

the wall will part
I will enter heaven in muddy shoes

I will come to the table
and answer questions rudely

I am all right leave me
alone. Head in hand I
sit and sit. How can I tell them
about that long
and tangled way.

Here in heaven mothers
knit green scarves

flies buzz

Father dozes by the stove
after six days' labour.

No – surely I can't tell them
that people are at each
other's throats.

Tadeusz Różewicz
(Translated by Adam Czerniawski)

Second Generation

Almost a Love Poem

If my parents and your parents
hadn't migrated to Eretz Yisrael in 1936,
we would have met in 1944

there, on the platform at Auschwitz.
I at twenty,
and you, at five.

Where's Mammele?
Where's Tattele?

What's your name?
Hannale.

Yehuda Amichai
(Translated by Glenda Abramson)

Draft of a Reparations Agreement

All right, gentlemen who cry blue murder as always,
nagging miracle-makers,
quiet!
Everything will be returned to its place,
paragraph after paragraph.
The scream back into the throat.
The gold teeth back to the gums.
The terror.
The smoke back to the tin chimney and further on and inside
back to the hollow of the bones,
and already you will be covered with skin and sinews and you
    will live,
look, you will have your lives back,
sit in the living room, read the evening paper.
Here you are. Nothing is too late.
As to the yellow star: immediately
it will be torn from your chest
and will emigrate
to the sky.

Dan Pagis
(Translated by Stephen Mitchell)

I Was Not There

The morning they set out from home
I was not there to comfort them
the dawn was innocent with snow
in mockery – it is not true
the dawn was neutral was immune
their shadows threaded it too soon
they were relieved that it had come
I was not there to comfort them

One told me that my father spent
a day in prison long ago
he did not tell me that he went
what difference does it make now
when he set out when he came home
I was not there to comfort him
and now I have no means to know
of what I was kept ignorant

Both my parents died in camps
I was not there to comfort them
I was not there they were alone
my mind refuses to conceive
the life the death they must have known
I must atone because I live
I could not have saved them from death
the ground is neutral underneath

Every child must leave its home
time gathers life impartially
I could have spared them nothing since
I was too young – it is not true
they might have lived to succour me
and none shall say in my defence
had I been there to comfort them
it would have made no difference

Karen Gershon

When It Happened

I was playing, I suppose,
when it happened.
No sound reached me.
The skies did not darken,
or if they did, one flicked
away the impression:
a cloud no doubt, a shadow perhaps
from those interminable aeroplanes
crossing and recrossing our
sunbleached beaches, Carbis Bay
or the Battery Rocks, where
all summer long we had dived
and cavorted in and out of
the tossing waters, while
the attention of the adults,
perpetually talking,
seemed focused,
unaccountably,
elsewhere.

No sound reached me
when it happened
over there on that
complicated frontier
near Geneva. (Was the sun
shining there too?)
I did not hear you cry out,
nor feel your heart thump wildly
in shock and terror. 'Go back,'
they shouted, those black-clad figures.
'Go back. You are not permitted to cross.'
Did the colour drain from your face?
Did your legs weaken?
'You are under arrest,' they barked.
'Go back and wait.' Back to the

crowd waiting for the train, the train. . .East?
Did you know what it meant?
Did you believe the rumours?
Were you silent? Stunned? Angry?

Did you signal to them then,
When it happened?
To the welcoming committee
one might say, on the other
side of the border.
To your husband and his friends
just a few yards away,
there, beyond the barbed wire,
beyond the notices saying,
'Illegal refugees will be shot.'
They called across, they said,
'Run, jump, take the risk,'
the frontier is such a thin line,
the distance so short between you and us,
between life and death,
(they said afterwards).
How was it you lacked
the courage (they said
afterwards, drinking tea).

No sound whatsoever disturbed me
when it happened.
I slept well. School
Was the same as usual.
As usual I went swimming,
or raced down the hill
on my scooter or on foot
laughing with friends.
Often at night
in the dark of my bed,
I would hear the trains being
shunted down at the station,

their anguished whistling
stirring my imagination,
drawing me towards oblivion.
At last, no more embarrassing letters
arrived in a foreign language
witnessing my alienation
from the cricketing scene.

Distracted and displaced
when it happened
I did not hear you ask
which cattle truck to mount,
nor, parched in the darkened
wagon, notice you beg for
a sip of water. On the third day,
perceiving the sound of Polish voices,
I did not catch you whisper to your neighbour,
'It is the East. We have arrived.'
Nor, naked and packed tight
with a hundred others
did I hear you choking
on the contents of those well-known
canisters marked 'Zyklon B Gas'.
(It took twelve minutes, they say.)
I was not listening
when it happened.

Now I hear nothing else.

Hilda Schiff

I Keep Forgetting

I keep forgetting
the facts and statistics
and each time
I need to know them

I look up books
these books line
twelve shelves
in my room

I know where to go
to confirm the fact
that in the Warsaw Ghetto
there were 7.2 people per room

and in Lodz
they allocated
5.8 people
to each room

I forget
over and over again
that one third of Warsaw
was Jewish

and in the ghetto
they crammed 500,000 Jews
into 2.4 per cent
of the area of the city

and how many
bodies they were burning
in Auschwitz
at the peak of their production

twelve thousand a day
I have to check
and re-check

and did I dream
that at 4pm on the 19th January
58,000 emaciated inmates
were marched out of Auschwitz

was I right
to remember that in Bergen Belsen
from the 4th-13th of April 1945
28,000 Jews arrived from other camps

I can remember
hundreds and hundreds
of phone numbers

phone numbers
I haven't phoned
for twenty years
are readily accessible

and I can remember
people's conversations
and what someone's wife
said to someone else's husband

what a good memory
you have
people tell me.

Lily Brett

Leaving You

It has taken me
a long time to know
that it was your war
not mine

that I wasn't
in Auschwitz
myself

that I have never
seen
the Lodz Ghetto

or Stuthof
or a cattle wagon
or a selection queue

I thought
I knew
Nazis

I thought
I had lived
with fear

with
ration cards
with work permits

I thought I knew
what bodies gnawed by rats
looked like

and how
the mattresses
smelt

and what
it felt like
to fill your lungs

with
smoke
from flesh

to
live
with death

I have had
trouble
Mother
leaving you.

Lily Brett

Holocaust 1944

To my mother

I do not know
In what strange far off earth
They buried you;
Nor what harsh northern winds
Blow through the stubble,
The dry, hard stubble
Above your grave.

And did you think of me
That frost-blue December morning,
Snow-heavy and bitter,
As you walked naked and shivering
Under the leaden sky,
In that last moment
When you knew it was the end,
The end of nothing
And the beginning of nothing,
Did you think of me?

Oh I remember you my dearest,
Your pale hands spread
In the ancient blessing
Your eyes bright and shining
Above the candles
Intoning the blessing
Blessed be the Lord. . . .

And therein lies the agony,
The agony and the horror
That after all there was no martyrdom
But only futility –
The futility of dying
The end of nothing
And the beginning of nothing.
I weep red tears of blood.
Your blood.

Anne Ranasinghe

The Book of Yolek

Wir Haben ein Gesetz,
Und nach dem Gesetz soll er sterben. *

The dowsed coals fume and hiss after your meal
Of grilled brook trout, and you saunter off for a walk
Down the fern trail. It doesn't matter where to,
Just so you're weeks and worlds away from home,
And among midsummer hills have set up camp
In the deep bronze glories of declining day.

You remember, peacefully, an earlier day
In childhood, remember a quite specific meal:
A corn roast and bonfire in summer camp.
That summer you got lost on a Nature Walk;
More than you dared admit, you thought of home:
No one else knows where the mind wanders to.

The fifth of August, 1942.
It was the morning and very hot. It was the day
They came at dawn with rifles to The Home
For Jewish Children, cutting short the meal
Of bread and soup, lining them up to walk
In close formation off to a special camp.

How often you have thought about that camp,
As though in some strange way you were driven to,
And about the children, and how they were made to walk,
Yolek who had bad lungs, who wasn't a day
Over five years old, commanded to leave his meal
And shamble between armed guards to his long home.

* We have a law, and according to the law he must die.

We're approaching August again. It will drive home
The regulation torments of that camp
Yolek was sent to, his small, unfinished meal,
The electric fences, the numeral tattoo,
The quite extraordinary heat of the day
They all were forced to take that terrible walk.

Whether on a silent, solitary walk
Or among crowds, far off or safe at home,
You will remember, helplessly, that day,
And the smell of smoke, and the loudspeakers of the camp.
Wherever you are, Yolek will be there, too.
His unuttered name will interrupt your meal.

Prepare to receive him in your home some day.
Though they killed him in the camp they sent him to,
He will walk in as you're sitting down to a meal.

Anthony Hecht

Daddy

You do not do, you do not do
Any more, black shoe
In which I have lived like a foot
For thirty years, poor and white,
Barely daring to breathe or Achoo.

Daddy, I have had to kill you.
You died before I had time –
Marble-heavy, a bag full of God,
Ghastly statue with one grey toe
Big as a Frisco seal

And a head in the freakish Atlantic
Where it pours bean green over blue
In the waters off beautiful Nauset.
I used to pray to recover you.
Ach, du.

In the German tongue, in the Polish town
Scraped flat by the roller
Of wars, wars, wars.
But the name of the town is common.
My Polack friend

Says there are a dozen or two.
So I never could tell where you
Put your foot, your root,
I never could talk to you.
The tongue stuck in my jaw.

It stuck in a barb wire snare.
Ich, ich, ich, ich,
I could hardly speak.
I thought every German was you.
And the language obscene

An engine, an engine
Chuffing me off like a Jew.
A Jew to Dachau, Auschwitz, Belsen.
I began to talk like a Jew.
I think I may well be a Jew.

The snows of the Tyrol, the clear beer of Vienna
Are not very pure or true.
With my gypsy ancestress and my weird luck
And my Taroc pack and my Taroc pack
I may be a bit of a Jew.

I have always been scared of *you*,
With your Luftwaffe, your gobbledygoo.
And your neat moustache
And your Aryan eye, bright blue.
Panzer-man, panzer-man, O You –

Not God but a swastika
So black no sky could squeak through.
Every woman adores a Fascist,
The boot in the face, the brute
Brute heart of a brute like you.

You stand at the blackboard, daddy,
In the picture I have of you,
A cleft in your chin instead of your foot
But no less a devil for that, no not
Any less the black man who

Bit my pretty red heart in two.
I was ten when they buried you.
At twenty I tried to die
And get back, back, back to you.
I thought even the bones would do.

But they pulled me out of the sack,
And they stuck me together with glue.
And then I knew what to do.
I made a model of you,
A man in black with a Meinkampf look

And a love of the rack and the screw.
And I said I do, I do.
So daddy, I'm finally through.
The black telephone's off at the root,
The voices just can't worm through.

If I've killed one man, I've killed two –
The vampire who said he was you
And drank my blood for a year,
Seven years, if you want to know.
Daddy, you can lie back now.

There's a stake in your fat black heart
And the villagers never liked you.
They are dancing and stamping on you.
They always *knew* it was you.
Daddy, daddy, you bastard, I'm through.

Sylvia Plath

Against Parting

My tailor is against parting.
That's why, he
said, he's not going away;
he doesn't want to part
from his only daughter. He's definitely
against parting.

Once, he parted from his wife
and he never did see her
after this (Auschwitz).
Parted
from his three sisters and
these he never again
looked upon (Buchenwald).
He once parted from his mother (his father
died at a ripe old age). Now
he's against parting.

In Berlin he was
my father's close companion. They passed
a good time in
that Berlin. The time passed. Now
he'll never go away. He's
most definitely
(my father died meanwhile)
against parting.

> Natan Zach
> (Translated by Peter Everwine &
> Shulamit Yasny-Starkman)

Lessons

Annotations of Auschwitz

I

When the burnt flesh is finally at rest,
The fires in the asylum grates will come up
And wicks turn down to darkness in the madman's eyes.

II

My suit is hairy, my carpet smells of death,
My toothbrush handle grows a cuticle.
I have six million foulnesses of breath.
Am I mad? The doctor holds my testicles
While the room fills with the Zyklon B I cough.

III

On Piccadilly underground I fall asleep –
I shuffle with the naked to the steel door,
Now I am only ten from the front – I wake up –
We are past Gloucester Rd, I am not a Jew,
But scratches web the ceiling of the train.

IV

Around staring buildings the pale flowers grow;
The frenetic butterfly, the bee made free by work,
Rouse and rape the pollen pads, the nectar stoops.
The rusting railway ends here. The blind end in Europe's gut.
Touch one piece of unstrung barbed wire –
Let it taste blood; let one man scream in pain.

V

A man eating his dressing in the hospital
Is lied to by his stomach. It's a final feast to him
Of beef blood pudding and black bread.
The orderly can't bear to see this mimic face
With its prim accusing picture after death.
On the stiff square a thousand bodies
Dig up useless ground – he hates them all,
These lives ignoble as ungoverned glands.
They fatten in statistics everywhere
And with their sick, unkillable fear of death
They crowd out peace from executioners' sleep.

VI

Forty thousand bald men drowning in a stream –
The like of light on all those bobbing skulls
Has never been seen before. Such death, says the painter,
Is worthwhile – it makes a colour never known.
It makes a sight that's unimagined, says the poet.
It's nothing to do with me, says the man who hates
The poet and the painter. Six million deaths can hardly
Occur at once. What do they make? Perhaps
An idiot's normalcy. I need never feel afraid
When I salt the puny snail – cruelty's grown up
And waits for time and men to bring into its hands
The snail's adagio and all the taunting life
Which has not cared about or guessed its tortured scope.

VII

London is full of chickens on electric spits,
    Cooking in windows where the public pass.
This, say the chickens, is their Auschwitz,
    And all poultry eaters are psychopaths.

Peter Porter

If

If Auschwitz had been in Hampshire
There would have been Englishmen to guard it
To administer records
Marshall transports
Work the gas ovens
And keep silent
The smoke would have drifted over these green hills

It's not that all men are evil or creatures of instinct
We – even our subjective self – are products of history
Of political change
In history two things join
Our will and things beyond our will
We change what we are as a means of controlling these things
That is: we create a new culture
We remain human only by changing
Each generation must create its own humanity

And the smoke will drift over these green hills
Our culture makes us barbarians
It does not allow us to live humanely
We must create a new culture
Or cease to be human

Edward Bond

How We See

After Treblinka
And the *spezialkommando*
Who tore a child with bare hands
Before its mother in Warsaw
We see differently.

Men taken from workshops and farms to fight for kaiser and
    king
Lived in a world asleep in mist
The *spezialkommando* lived in a world of electric lights cinemas
    planes and radios
We see racist slogans chalked on walls differently
We see walls differently

Edward Bond

The Survivor

I am twenty-four
led to slaughter
I survived.

The following are empty synonyms:
man and beast
love and hate
friend and foe
darkness and light.

The way of killing men and beasts is the same
I've seen it:
truckfuls of chopped-up men
who will not be saved.

Ideas are mere words:
virtue and crime
truth and lies
beauty and ugliness
courage and cowardice.

Virtue and crime weigh the same
I've seen it:
in a man who was both
criminal and virtuous.

I seek a teacher and a master
may he restore my sight hearing and speech
may he again name objects and ideas
may he separate darkness from light.

I am twenty-four
led to slaughter
I survived.

Tadeusz Różewicz
(Translated by Adam Czerniawski)

In the Midst of Life

After the end of the world
after death
I found myself in the midst of life
creating myself
building life
people animals landscapes

this is a table I said
this is a table
there is bread and a knife on the table
knife serves to cut bread
people are nourished by bread

man must be loved
I learnt by night by day
what must one love
I would reply man

this is a window I said
this is a window
there is a garden beyond the window
I see an apple-tree in the garden
the apple-tree blossoms
the blossom falls
fruit is formed
ripens

my father picks the apple
the man who picks the apple
is my father

I sat on the threshold
that old woman who
leads a goat on a string
is needed more
is worth more

than the seven wonders of the world
anyone who thinks or feels
she is not needed
is a mass murderer

this is a man
this is a tree this is bread

people eat to live
I kept saying to myself
human life is important
human life has great importance
the value of life
is greater than the value of all things
which man has created
man is a great treasure
I repeated stubbornly

this is water I said
I stroked the waves with my hand
and talked to the river
water I would say
nice water
this is me

man talked to water
talked to the moon
to the flowers and to rain
talked to the earth
to the birds
to the sky

the sky was silent
the earth was silent
and if a voice was heard
flowing
from earth water and sky
it was a voice of another man

Tadeusz Różewicz

Race

When I returned to my home town
believing that no one would care
who I was and what I thought
it was as if the people caught
an echo of me everywhere
they knew my story by my face
and I who am always alone
became a symbol of my race

Like every living Jew I have
in imagination seen
the gas-chamber the mass-grave
the unknown body which was mine
and found in every German face
behind the mask the mark of Cain
I will not make their thoughts my own
by hating people for their race

Karen Gershon

Synagogue in Prague

Killers said
Before they used their slide-rules
'Death is the way to Freedom':
Seventy-seven thousand names
Carved on these great walls
Are a gaol Death cannot open.

Eyes close in awe and sorrow
As if that name was my mother
That boy starved to death my son
Those men gassed my brothers
Or striving cousins.

It might have been me and if it was
I spend a day searching the words
For my name.
I'd be glad it was not me
If the dead could see sky again,
Reach that far-off river and swim in it.

What can one say
When shouting rots the brain?
The dead god hanging in churches
Was not allowed to hear
Of work calling for revenge
To ease the pain of having let it happen
And stop it being planned again.

Letters calling for revenge on such a wall
Would vandalize that encyphered synagogue,
And seventy-seven thousand
Stonily indented names
Would still show through.

Vengeance is Jehovah's own;
To prove He's not abandoned us
He gave the gift of memory,
The fruit of all trees
In the Land of Israel.

Alan Sillitoe

During the Eichmann Trial

When we look up
each from his being
Robert Duncan

He had not looked,
pitiful man whom none

pity, whom all
must pity if they look

into their own face (given
only by glass, steel, water

barely known) all
who look up

to see – how many
faces? How many

seen in a lifetime? (Not those
that flash by, but those

into which the gaze wanders
and is lost

and returns to tell
Here is a mystery,

a person, an
other, an I?

Count them.
Who are five million?)

'I was used from the nursery
to obedience

all my life . . .
Corpselike

obedience.' Yellow
calmed him later –

'a charming picture'
yellow of autumn leaves in

Wienerwald, a little
railroad station
nineteen-o-eight, Lemburg,

yellow sun
on the stepmother's teatable

Franz Joseph's beard
blessing his little ones.

It was the yellow
of the stars too,

stars that marked
those in whose faces

you had not
looked. 'They were cast out

as if they were
some animals, some beasts.'

'And what would disobedience
have brought me? And

whom would it have served?'
'I did not let my thoughts

dwell on this – I had
seen it and that was

enough.' (The words
'slur into a harsh babble')

'A spring of blood
gushed from the earth.'
Miracle

unsung. I see
a spring of blood gush from the earth –

Earth cannot swallow
so much at once

a fountain
rushes towards the sky

unrecognized
a sign – .

Pity this man who saw it
whose obedience continued –

he, you, I, which shall I say?
He stands

isolate in a bulletproof
witness-stand of glass,

a cage, where we may view
ourselves, an apparition

telling us something he
does not know: we are members

one of another.

Denise Levertov

Campo dei Fiori

In Rome, on Campo dei Fiori,
baskets of olives and lemons
cobbles spattered with wine
and the wreckage of flowers.
Vendors cover the trestles
with rose-pink fish;
armfuls of dark grapes
heaped on peach-down.

On this same square
they burned Giordano Bruno.
Henchmen kindled the pyre
close-pressed by the mob.
Before the flames had died
the taverns were full again,
baskets of olives and lemons
again on the vendors' shoulders.

I thought of Campo dei Fiori
In Warsaw by the sky-carrousel
one clear spring evening
to the strains of a carnival tune.
The bright melody drowned
the salvos from the ghetto wall
and couples were flying
High in the blue sky.

At times wind from the burning
would drift dark kites along
and riders on the carrousel
caught petals in midair.
That same hot wind
blew open the skirts of the girls
and the crowds were laughing
on the beautiful Warsaw Sunday.

Someone will read a moral
that the people of Rome and Warsaw
haggle, laugh, make love
as they pass by martyrs' pyres.
Someone else will read
of the passing of things human,
of the oblivion
born before the flames have died.

But that day I thought only
of the loneliness of the dying,
of how, when Giordano
climbed to his burning
he could not find
in any human tongue
words for mankind,
mankind who live on.

Already they were back at their wine
or peddled their white starfish,
baskets of olives and lemons
they had shouldered to the fair,
and he already distanced
as if centuries had passed
while they paused just a moment
for his flying in the fire.

Those dying here, the lonely
forgotten by the world,
our tongue becomes for them
the language of an ancient planet.
Until, when all is legend
and many years have passed,
on a new Campo dei Fiori
rage will kindle at a poet's word.

Czeslaw Milosz

Posthumous Rehabilitation

The dead have remembered
our indifference
The dead have remembered
our silence
The dead have remembered
our words

The dead see our snouts
laughing from ear to ear
The dead see
our bodies rubbing against each other
The dead hear
clucking tongues

The dead read our books
listen to our speeches
delivered so long ago

The dead scrutinize our lectures
join in previously terminated
discussions
The dead see our hands
poised for applause

The dead see stadiums
ensembles and choirs declaiming rhythmically

all the living are guilty

little children
who offered bouquets of flowers
are guilty
lovers are guilty
guilty are poets

guilty are those who ran away
and those that stayed
those who were saying yes
those who said no
and those who said nothing

the dead are taking stock of the living
the dead will not rehabilitate us

Tadeusz Różewicz
(Translated by Adam Czerniawski)

May, 1945

As the Allied tanks trod Germany to shard
and no man had seen a fresh-pressed uniform
for six months, as the fire storm
bit out the core of Dresden yard by yard,

as farmers hid turnips for the after-war,
as cadets going to die passed Waffen SS
tearing identifications from their battledress,
the Russians only three days from the Brandenburger Tor –

in the very hell of sticks and blood and brick dust
as Germany the phoenix burned, the wraith
of History pursed its lips and spoke, thus:

To go with teeth and toes and human soap,
the radio will broadcast Bruckner's Eighth
so that good and evil may die in equal hope.

Peter Porter

War Has Been Given a Bad Name

I am told that the best people have begun saying
How, from a moral point of view, the Second World War
Fell below the standard of the First. The *Wehrmacht*
Allegedly deplores the methods by which the SS effected
The extermination of certain peoples. The Ruhr industrialists
Are said to regret the bloody manhunts
Which filled their mines and factories with slave workers.
   The intellectuals
So I heard, condemn industry's demand for slave workers
Likewise their unfair treatment. Even the bishops
Dissociate themselves from this way of waging war; in short
   the feeling
Prevails in every quarter that the Nazis did the Fatherland
A lamentably bad turn, and that war,
While in itself natural and necessary, has, thanks to the
Unduly ininhibited and positively inhuman
Way in which it was conducted on this occasion, been
Discredited for some time to come.

Bertolt Brecht
(Translated by John Willet)

Portrait of a House Detective

he lolls in the supermarket
under the plastic sun,
the white patches on his face
are rage, not consumption,
a hundred packets of crispy crackers
(*because they're so nourishing*)
he sets ablaze with his eyes,
a piece of margarine
(the same brand as mine:
goldlux, because it's so delicious)
he picks up with his moist hand
and squeezes it till it drips.

he's twenty-nine,
idealistic,
sleeps badly and alone
with pamphlets and blackheads,
hates the boss and the supermarket,
communists, women,
landlords, himself
and his bitten fingernails
full of margarine (*because
it's so delicious*), under
his arty hairstyle mutters
to himself like a pensioner.

that one
will never get anywhere.
wittler, I think, he's called,
wittler, hittler, or something like that.

Hans Magnus Enzenberger
(Translated by Michael Hamburger)

Riddle

From Belsen a crate of gold teeth,
from Dachau a mountain of shoes,
from Auschwitz a skin lampshade,
Who killed the Jews?

Not I, cries the typist,
Not I, cries the engineer,
Not I, cries Adolf Eichmann,
Not I, cries Albert Speer.

My friend Fritz Nova lost his father –
a petty official had to choose.
My friend Lou Abrahms lost his brother.
Who killed the Jews?

David Nova swallowed gas,
Hyman Abrahms was beaten and starved.
Some men signed their papers,
and some stood guard,

and some herded them in,
and some dropped the pellets,
and some spread the ashes,
and some hosed the walls,

and some planted the wheat,
and some poured the steel,
and some cleared the rails,
and some raised the cattle.

Some smelled the smoke,
some just heard the news.
Were they Germans? Were they Nazis?
Were they human? Who killed the Jews?

The stars will remember the gold,
the sun will remember the shoes,
the moon will remember the skin.
But who killed the Jews?

William Heyen

Annus Mirabilis 1989

Ten years ago, beneath the Hotel Astoria,
we watched a dissident cabaret in Budapest,
where they showed Einstein as a Jewish tailor.
All the women on stage were elegantly dressed.

Their silken garments were cleverly slit to expose
illicit glimpses of delicate thighs and breast.
Einstein was covered with chalk, in ill-fitting clothes;
he was taking measurements, trying to please the rest.

At the climax of the play, to applause and laughter
they raked him with strobe lights and the noise of guns.
I was chilled by the audience euphoria.
Of course, I don't have a word of Hungarian,

and afterwards there were embarrassed explanations,
which left out tailoring and obsequious gestures.
Their indignation was all about nuclear science, while
I pondered at the resilience of an old monster.

Elaine Feinstein

God

(i)

Smoke Rose

Smoke
rose
  in the garden.
God watched
from above,
and fear walked
in the cool
  of the day.

      Itamar Yaoz-Kest
        (Translated by
      Glenda Abramson)

Written In Pencil in the Sealed Freightcar

Here in this carload
I am Eve
With my son Abel
If you see my older boy
Cain son of Adam
Tell him that I

Dan Pagis
(Translated Stephen Mitchell)

Zürich, the Stork Inn

For Nelly Sachs

Of too much was our talk, of
too little. Of the You
and You-Again, of
how clarity troubles, of
Jewishness, of
your God.

Of
that.
On the day of an ascension, the
Minister stood over there, it sent
some gold across the water.

Of your God was our talk, I spoke
against him, I
let the heart that I had
hope:
for
his highest, death-rattled, his
quarrelling word –

Your eye looked on, looked away,
your mouth
spoke its way to the eye, and I heard:

We
don't know, you know,
we
don't know, do we?
what
counts.

Paul Celan
(Translated by Michael Hamburger)

Who Am I?

Who am I? They often tell me
I would step from my cell's confinement
Calmly, cheerfully, firmly,
Like a squire from his country-house.

Who am I? They often tell me
I would talk to my warders
Freely and friendly and clearly,
As though it were mine to command.

Who am I? They also tell me
I would bear the days of misfortune
Equably, smilingly, proudly,
Like one accustomed to win.

Am I then really all that which other men tell of?
Or am I only what I know of myself?
Restless and longing and sick, like a bird in a cage,
Struggling for breath, as though hands were compressing my
      throat,
Yearning for colours, for flowers, for the voices of birds,
Thirsting for words of kindness, for neighbourliness,
Tossing in expectation of great events,
Powerlessly trembling for friends at an infinite distance,
Weary and empty at praying, at thinking, at making,
Faint, and ready to say farewell to it all?

Who am I? This or the other?
Am I one person today and tomorrow another?
Am I both at once? A hypocrite before others,
And before myself a contemptibly woebegone weakling?
Or is something within me still like a beaten army,
Fleeing in disorder from victory already achieved?

Who am I? They mock me, these lonely questions of mine.
Whoever I am, Thou knowest, O God, I am Thine!

Dietrich Bonhoeffer
(Translated by Reginald H. Fuller)

I Believe

I believe in the sun
though it is late
in rising

I believe in love
though it is absent

I believe in God
though he is
silent. . . .

(Translated from the French by the editor. Text from an unsigned inscription found on the wall of a cave in Cologne where Jews had been hiding.)

What Luck

What luck I can pick
berries in the wood
I thought
there is no wood no berries.

What luck I can lie
in the shade of a tree
I thought trees
no longer give shade.

What luck I am with you
my heart beats so
I thought man
has no heart.

Tadeusz Różewicz
(Translated by Adam Czerniawski)

Without Jews

Without Jews, no Jewish God.
If, God forbid, we should quit
this world, Your poor tent's light
would out.
Abraham knew You in a cloud:
since then, You are the flame
of our face, the rays
our eyes blaze,
our likeness
whom we formed:
in every land and town
a stranger.
Shattered Jewish skulls,
shards of the divine,
smashed, shamed pots –
these were Your light-bearing vessels,
Your tangibles,
Your portents of miracle!
Now count these heads
by the millions of the dead.
Around You the stars go dark.
Our memory of You, obscured.
Soon Your reign will close.
Where Jews sowed,
a scorched waste.

Dews weep
on dead grass.
The dream raped,
reality raped,
both blotted out.
Whole congregations sleep,
the babies, the women,
the young, the old.
Even Your pillars, Your rocks,
the tribe of Your saints,*
sleep their dead
eternal sleep.

Who will dream You?
Remember You?
Deny You?
Yearn after You?
Who will flee You,
only to return
over a bridge of longing?

No end to night
for an extinguished people.
Heaven and earth wiped out.
Your tent void of light.
Flicker of the Jews' last hour.
Soon, Jewish God,
Your eclipse.

Jacob Glatstein
(Translated by Cynthia Ozick)

* Refers to the legend of the last 36 Just Men for whose sake the world is
  saved.

Experiments with God

As a child before she knew
what it meant to be a Jew
she thought that God was on her side
when she was starved when she was stoned
deprived of everything she owned
she felt chosen and was proud
but she was without defence
against God's indifference

From the garbage bin of death
she took the evidence to God
growing articulate beneath
her proliferating load
contaminated by decay
she kept the scavengers at bay
with words till she was silenced by
the gas of Auschwitz on God's breath

Karen Gershon

The Jugs

At the long tables of time
The jugs of God carouse.
They drink empty the eyes that see
              and the eyes of the blind,
the hearts of the mastering shadows,
the hollow cheek of the evening.
They are the most mighty carousers:
they carry empty and full alike to their mouths
and do not flow over like you or like me.

Paul Celan
(Translated by Christopher Middleton)

Psalm

No one moulds us again out of earth and clay,
no one conjures our dust.
No one.

Praised be your name, no one.
For your sake
we shall flower.
Towards
you.

A nothing
we were, are, shall
remain, flowering:
the nothing-, the
no one's rose.

With
our pistil soul-bright,
with our stamen heaven-ravaged,
our corolla red
with the crimson word which we sang
over, O over
the thorn.

Paul Celan
(Translated by Michael Hamburger)

After Auschwitz

Anger,
as black as a hook,
overtakes me.
Each day,
each Nazi
took, at 8.00 a.m., a baby
and sautéed him for breakfast
in his frying pan.

And death looks on with a casual eye
and picks at the dirt under his fingernail.

Man is evil,
I say aloud.
Man is a flower
that should be burnt,
I say aloud.
Man
is a bird full of mud,
I say aloud.

And death looks on with a casual eye
and scratches his anus.

Man with his small pink toes,
with his miraculous fingers
is not a temple
but an outhouse,
I say aloud.
Let man never again raise his teacup.
Let man never again write a book.
Let man never again put on his shoe.
Let man never again raise his eyes,
on a soft July night.
Never. Never. Never. Never. Never.
I say these things aloud.

I beg the Lord not to hear.

Anne Sexton

Discovery

I have found God
In the sulphurous darkness of absolute negation.

An endless brick wall, close-packed and blank
Are his eyes.

I hear his mindless inscrutable voice in
Shapeless silence.

When my brothers walk through the gas-chambers of Auschwitz
I know his sanctuary

In their boots blithely kicking the screaming infant
Helpless to evil

Far beyond frontiers of man's imagining and football games
Of judgement-making.

The total absence of love is God
Whose presence

No clearer moments of rapture could stamp in the
Grain of my heart.

Yet his wings of meaning beat impotently patient
Against the opaque

Of my racked
Rejection. I wait in the dense air of living

for the lightning

conductor

of death

Hilda Schiff

from *Ani Maamin,*
A Song Lost and Found Again*

Behold, God of Abraham, God of mercy,
Open your eyes as you have opened mine,
Open your eyes and see what I have seen.

Jacob: I remember a dream,
A dream I had, long ago.
At Beth-El.
A dream magnificent and symbolic:
See the immense ladder, a bridge to the sky.
An entire people,
Mine, yours,
Uses it to rise,
To vanish in the clouds.

~

You promised me so many things, my Lord.
You promised me to watch over Israel –
Where are you? What of your promise?
You promised me blessings for Israel –
Is this your blessing?
Behold, O Lord:

~

Narrator: And Jacob began to weep. And so did Abraham.
And Isaac. And all the angels, all the seraphim from
all the heavens joined in their weeping.

But not God. He alone remained calm. Unmoved.
Silent.

---

* A dramatic poem set to music by Darius Milhaud, based on the *Hebrew Prayer: I believe in the coming of the Messiah.*

Abraham: You commanded me, O Lord,
                In the beginning,
                The very beginning,
                To leave my country,
                My home,
                And that of my father.
                To start anew in the land of Canaan.
                I did not know, my Lord, I did not know
                That one day, one night,
                The road would end in Treblinka.

Isaac: You made me climb, then descend
                Mount Moriah –
                Crushed and silent.
                I did not know, my Lord, I did not know
                It was to see my children,
                Old and young,
                Arrive in Majdanek.

Jacob: You brought my descendants home –
                I did not know, my Lord, I did not know then,
                That every road
                At dusk
                Would lead to Auschwitz.

Chorus: Pray for Abraham in Treblinka.
                Pray for Isaac in Majdanek.
                Pray for Jacob in Auschwitz.
                Pray for those who pray,
                And for those, also,
                Who are too weak
                To pray.

Abraham: Warsaw.
          A bunker.
          A widow and the last
          Of her five sons. An infant
          But a few months old.
          Wide-eyed,
          Trembling,
          She implores her companions
          Not to be angry
          With her crying son,
          Too small to understand
          He must not cry.
          He is hungry, the little boy,
          He is thirsty.
          He hurts, he gasps for air,
          Flails his arms,
          Makes noise.
          Not too much,
          Just enough,
          Which is too much.
          Suddenly, steps.
          Raucous shouting.
          The killers are coming closer.
          The occupants of the bunker,
          Their nails dug into their palms,
          Hold their breath.
          Even the infant is silent for a moment.
          Only for a moment.
          Then he begins to cry again.
          From the four corners
          Of the bunker,
          Anxious, angry whispers
          Reach the mother:
          Keep him quiet!
          For the love of heaven,
          Keep him still!
          The woman,

Her throat parched,
Caresses the frail head
Of the last of her five sons.
She would like to soothe him,
Save him.
In vain.
He cries and cries.
And then,
In the dark,
A hand is raised.
An arm inches forward,
Closer –
The hand, the arm
Of a madman perhaps,
Surely desperate.
Then
There is silence.
Total, absolute silence.
Yet – the death of the child
Fails to save the others.
It is simply the first of many.
But I saw the mother.
The shudder that went through her.
I offer you that shudder.
I saw her gaze fill with madness.
I offer you that madness
As I offer you her gaze.

Isaac: A forest,
One spring morning.
Surrounded by killers
And their dogs,
Jews from the nearby village
March towards death.
There are those
Who have guessed
But say nothing –

And those
Who have chosen self-delusion.
A beautiful day.
The sun plays
In the branches.
A bird sings
Of the joy of song;
Another responds.
In the crowd of the condemned,
An old man
And his son.
They speak
In a low voice.
The father believes in miracles:
Anything can happen,
Even at the last moment,
If only God wills it.
Avoiding his son's gaze,
He tells him
That now,
More than ever,
One may not despair.

Chorus: Hear, O God.
O God, answer.
On behalf of Abraham,
Isaac,
And Jacob,
On behalf of your defenders,
Your children implore you:
Hear and answer!

Narrator: But heaven is silent, and its silence is a wall.

Chorus: Abraham has spoken:
Heed him.
Isaac has cried out:

Answer him.
Jacob has wept:
Receive his tears.

God of silence, speak.
God of cruelty, smile.
God of the word, answer.
Just God, unjust God,
Judge the word and judge the deed,
Judge the crime and judge the tool.
God present, God absent,
You are in everything,
Even in evil.
You are in everything,
Above all, in man.
God present, God absent,
Where are you
On this night?

Abraham: A field.
Jewish mothers,
Naked,
Lead their naked children
To their sacrifice.
I see the priests,
Dressed in black,
Behind the machine guns,
And at the peepholes
Of special installations
In Birkenau and Treblinka.
But the mothers
See nothing.
I see them,
These mothers
And their little girls.
Gaunt, distraught mothers;
Tired, frightened children.

Clumsily, to no avail,
Some women try to hide
Their nakedness.
And I am looking.
Aching.
Going mad.
I snatch a little girl,
Blue eyes, black hair,
I snatch her from her mother
And I run.
I run
As far as my legs will carry me,
Like the wind,
With the wind,
Farther than the wind.
I run,
And while I run,
I am thinking:
This is insane,
This Jewish child
Will not be spared.
I run and run
And cry.
And while I am crying,
While I am running,
I perceive a whisper:
I believe,
Says the little girl,
Weakly,
I believe in you.

Chorus: *Ani maamin*, Abraham.
        I believe, Father,
        Forefather, I believe
        You will live within us,
        After us,
        Even if I,

Daughter of Sarah, Leah or Rachel,
Am the last survivor,
The last one living.
I believe in you,
I believe
In your mission,
In your faithfulness
I believe.

Jacob: A camp.
An inmate.
A creature without a name,
A man without a face,
Without a destiny.
It is night,
The first night of Passover.
The camp is asleep,
He alone is awake.
He talks to himself
Soundlessly.
I hear his words,
I capture his silence.
To himself, to me,
He is saying:
I have not partaken of *matzoth*,
Nor of *marror*.*
I have not emptied the four cups,
Symbols of the four deliverances.
I did not invite
The hungry
To share my repast –
Or even my hunger.
No longer have I a son
To ask me

* Unleavened bread [*matzoth*] and bitter herbs [*marror*] traditionally eaten at
the Passover meal.

The four questions –
No longer have I the strength
To answer.
I say the *Haggadah**
And I know it lies.
The parable of *Had-Gadya*† is false:
God will not come
To slay the slaughterer.
The innocent victims
Will go unavenged.
The ancient wish –
Leshana habaa bi-Yerushalaim‡ –
Will not be granted.

Still, I recite the *Haggadah*
As though I believe in it.
And I await the prophet Elijah,
As I did long ago.
I open my heart to him
And say:
Welcome, prophet of the promise,
Welcome, herald of redemption.
Come, share in my story,
Come, rejoice with the dead
That we are.
Empty the cup
That bears your name.
Come to us,
Come to us on this Passover night:

* The Biblical story of the Exodus from Egypt, exemplifying God's covenant
  with the Jewish people.
† A traditional, jolly song, 'Only One Kid', sung at the end of the Passover
  service.
‡ Next year in Jerusalem

We are in Egypt
And we are the ones
To suffer God's plagues.
Come, friend of the poor,
Defender of the oppressed,
Come.
I shall wait for you.
And even if you disappoint me
I shall go on waiting,
*Ani maamin.**

Chorus: *Ani maamin*, Abraham,
Despite Treblinka.
Ani maamin, Isaac,
Because of Belsen.
Ani maamin, Jacob,
Because and in spite of Majdanek.
Dead in vain,
Dead for naught,
Ani maamin.
Pray, men.
Pray to God,
Against God,
For God.
Ani maamin.
Whether the Messiah comes,
Ani maamin.
Or is late in coming,
Ani maamin.
Whether God is silent
Or weeps,
Ani maamin.
Ani maamin for him,
In spite of him.
I believe in you,

* I believe

Even against your will.
Even if you punish me
For believing in you.
Blessed are the fools
Who shout their faith.
Blessed are the fools
Who go on laughing,
Who mock the man who mocks the Jew,
Who help their brothers
Singing, over and over and over:
Ani maamin.
Ani maamin beviat ha-Mashiah,
Veaf al pi sheyitmameha,
Akhake lo bekhol yom sheyavo,
Ani maamin. *

Elie Wiesel

---

* I believe in the coming of the Messiah,/And though he tarries,/I wait daily
for his coming,/I believe.

Shemá*

You who live secure
In your warm houses,
Who return at evening to find
Hot food and friendly faces:

>Consider whether this is a man,
>Who labours in the mud
>Who knows no peace
>Who fights for a crust of bread
>Who dies at a yes or a no.
>Consider whether this is a woman,
>Without hair or name
>With no more strength to remember
>Eyes empty and womb cold
>As a frog in winter.

Consider that this has been:
I commend these words to you.
Engrave them on your hearts
When you are in your house, when you walk on your way,
When you go to bed, when you rise.
Repeat them to your children.
Or may your house crumble,
Disease render you powerless,
Your offspring avert their faces from you.

Primo Levi
(Translated by Ruth Feldman & Brian Swann)

---

* This poem is based on the principal Jewish prayer, 'Hear, [*Shemá*] O Israel, the Lord our God, the Lord is One' (Deuteronomy, 6:4–9; 11:13–21; Numbers 15:37–41). Primo Levi reworks some of its major ideas, making it possible to incorporate the experience of the Holocaust into the Jewish religion.

BIOGRAPHICAL DETAILS

Dannie **Abse,** poet and novelist, born in Cardiff, Wales, in 1923. He has published eight collections of poetry amongst other writings, and has a high reputation in the UK and elsewhere. See *Collected Poems, 1948–76,* 1977, and *Remembrance of Crimes Past, Poems 1986–89,* 1990.

Yehuda **Amichai,** Hebrew writer, born in Germany in 1924 and migrated to Israel in 1936. He saw active service both before and after the Israeli War of Independence. For many years he was a schoolteacher. He has published many volumes of poetry. His *Selected Poems,* in English translation, appeared in 1988, and his novel about the Holocaust, *Not of This Time, Not of This Place,* in 1981. He has been widely translated and is highly regarded in Israel and throughout the world.

W. H. **Auden,** poet and dramatist, born 1907. He began to make his mark while still at Oxford when T. S. Eliot, who was then at Faber and Faber, published his *Poems* in 1930. Auden, highly talented, dominated his friends such as Spender, Isherwood and MacNeice. He continued to publish verse and drama. In the late 1920s he lived in Berlin and saw the rise of Hitler, and in 1937 visited Spain. In 1939 he left Europe for America where he met the Jewish Chester Kallman, his lifelong companion. He continued to publish verse and drama prolifically, wrote increasingly of man's isolation, and seemed to turn towards Christianity. He spent his last years in Oxford and in Austria, where he died in 1973. See his *Selected Poems,* edited by Edward Mendelson, 1979.

Edward **Bond,** poet and dramatist, was born in 1934 in England and left school early. He has written a number of prominent controversial plays, such as *Saved,* 1965, some of them originally banned, all concerned with social injustice. In *Narrow Road to the Deep North*, 1968, he compares fascism with imperialism. He is less well known for his three volumes of poetry, see, for example, *Poems 1978–1985*, 1987.

Dietrich **Bonhoeffer,** German theologian, born 1906 in Breslau. He was strongly opposed to Hitler and the Nazi regime, and felt the established churches in Germany were tools in Hitler's hands. He became involved with Admiral Canaris's counter-espionage activities and also helped some Jews to escape to Switzerland. He was arrested on 5 April 1943 and in July imprisoned in the Gestapo cellars in Berlin. On 7 February 1945 he was sent to Buchenwald. He was shot on 9 April 1945, only a few weeks before the end of the war. See *Letters and Papers from Prison*, edited by Eberhard Bethge, 1970.

Tadeusz **Borowski,** Polish poet and prose writer, was born in 1922 in the Ukraine. He published poetry before and after the war, as well as several volumes of short stories set in concentration camps. Of these the only collection available in English translation is entitled *This Way for the Gas, Ladies and Gentlemen*, 1976. Borowski was imprisoned in Dachau and Auschwitz between 1943 and 1945 but survived by helping, in a very lowly capacity, to administer the death regimes in these institutions as did many other survivors. Borowski describes Auschwitz with the tortured detachment of a tragic artist. Having survived the war and given expression to his agonized view of the human condition, he committed suicide in 1951. (Compare Paul Celan and Primo Levi.) His poetry, simultaneously tragic and lyrical, is unavailable in the UK in any language.

Bertolt **Brecht** was born in Augsburg, Bavaria in 1891. He studied medicine and science. He became a Marxist in the late 1930s and, subject to persecution, fled from Nazi Germany. He found refuge in Denmark and Finland, and later spent some time in the USA. He became celebrated for his plays, *Mother Courage* most notably, and for his libretto (now not attributed to him alone) for Kurt Weill's *The Three-penny Opera*. After the defeat of Nazi Germany he returned to Berlin and founded the influential Berliner Ensemble theatre company. He wrote and published poetry extensively throughout his life, always seeking to express himself clearly and with apparent simplicity. He died in 1956. See *Collected Poems 1913–1956*, edited John Willet and Ralph Mannheim, 1976.

Lily **Brett,** poet and novelist. She was born in Germany after the war and migrated to Australia with her parents in 1948. Lily Brett has published five collections of poems and three volumes of fiction. See *The Auschwitz Poems*, 1986, and *After the War*, 1990, both published in Australia where her fiction and poetry have won major literary prizes. She now lives in New York.

Van K. **Brock,** American poet, born 1932 and brought up on a farm in Georgia. He writes of concentration camp inmates but is also interested in the experience of war-torn Germany. See *The Hard Essential Landscape*, 1969, and *Weighing the Penalties*, 1977, both USA.

Paul **Celan,** poet whose native tongue was German. He was born in Czernowitz, Bukovina, of Jewish parents, in 1920. His original name was Paul Ansel. In 1942 Celan saw his parents deported to Auschwitz. He himself survived in other camps but never recovered, and in 1970 committed suicide. (Compare Primo Levi and Tadeusz Borowski.) Celan's poetic output after the war received great acclaim in Germany where he was showered with literary prizes. His first collection of poems appeared in 1948, *Der Sand aus den Urnen* (Sand from Urns). He continued to publish until the end of his life. His poetry was translated into English, most notably by Michael Hamburger. See *Poems of Paul Celan*, 1988 and 1994. Celan's work is powerful, highly original, often ambiguous, and deeply tragic. His reputation as a poet of the Holocaust is second to none.

Hans Magnus **Enzenberger,** German poet, translator and editor, born 1929 in Kaufbeuren. As founder of the journal *Kursbuch*, he has been an influential literary figure in post-war Germany. His style in dealing with the self-centredness, superficiality and kitsch of modern consumerism is satirical and mocking. Amongst his other publications, see *Selected Poems*, 1968.

Ruth **Fainlight**, poet, short story writer and translator, born 1931 in New York. She has lived in the UK for over 35 years and has published nine collections of poems, from *Cages*, 1966, through *Selected Poems*, 1987, to *This Time of Year*, 1993.

Elaine **Feinstein,** poet, novelist and translator, born 1930 in Bootle and educated at Newnham College, Cambridge. Her many novels include *The Survivors*, 1982, a story about a Jewish immigrant family in Liverpool, and *The Dreamers*, 1994, set in Vienna. She has published a number of collections of poems.

James **Fenton**, poet, born 1949 in Lincoln and educated at Durham and Oxford where, as an undergraduate, he won the Newdigate Prize for poetry. He became a journalist, travelling to Germany and the Far East as a war reporter. His first collection of poems, *Terminal Moraine*, appeared in 1972; *The Memory of War and Children in Exile*, in 1983. He writes of the self-deception and ambiguity of Hitler's German contemporaries, but also of their silent suffering. In 1994 he became Professor of Poetry in Oxford.

Jerzy **Ficowski**, Polish poet, translator, literary critic. He was born in Poland in 1924. Ficowski fought in the Polish army in the war, and his work is particularly focused on the sufferings of the gypsies and the victims of the Holocaust in Poland. His poem 'Your two mothers' concerns the story of his wife who was smuggled out of the Warsaw Ghetto immediately she was born, and brought up by a fostermother. Her natural Jewish mother perished. It was not until 1981 that this underrated and deeply moving poet's work was translated into English by Keith Bosley and Krystyna Wandycz in *A Reading of Ashes*, 1981 published by the Menard Press.

Ephraim **Fogel**, author and scholar. Little is known of him apart from what is self-evident from his poem which is taken from Jon Stallworthy's *The Oxford Book of War Poetry*, 1984. Under Ephraim Fogel's name, the Library of Congress in Washington lists the following items: *A Concordance to the Poems of Ben Jonson*, Cornell University Press, 1978, and *The Odessy of Osip Mandelstam*, 1974, a sound recording made for the Society for the Humanities.

Pavel **Friedmann**, young poet and Theresienstadt inmate. Little is known of the author of this widely anthologized poem 'The Butterfly' marked 4-6-42. He is presumed to have been 17 years old when he wrote it, but it was found amongst a hidden cache of children's work recovered at the end of the war and deposited in the Jewish Museum of Prague. (Archive number 105.516, 1–8.) There were 15,000 children amongst the prisoners at Theresienstadt, and their poems and drawings display a desperate attempt to keep their spirits up. Only 100 of these children survived. Like most of the others, Pavel Friedmann was eventually deported to Auschwitz, and on 29 September 1944 died there. See *Children's Drawings & Poems from Theresienstadt Concentration Camp*, produced by Neville Spearman, London, 1965.

Karen **Gershon,** poet and prose writer, born in Bielefeld, Germany, in 1923. She was brought to England in 1939 without her family. She made a name for herself when she wrote *We Came As Children*, 1966. She was a pioneer in writing of her inner life as a German refugee in England, and her poems became well known in the 1960s and were widely anthologized. Unlike more sophisticated poets who sometimes used Holocaust imagery for other purposes (e.g. Sylvia Plath, Anne Sexton), Karen Gershon wrote in a straightforward way about the effects of the Holocaust on individuals, and of her unending grief for her parents who perished. See *Selected Poems*, 1966. She died in 1993.

Hayim **Gouri,** Hebrew poet, was born in 1923 in Israel. He served in the Palmach, the Haganah and in the Israeli Defence Forces. After the war he was sent to Europe where he visited Displaced Persons' Camps. He wrote of the ordeal of survivors in seeking to reconstruct their lives in the so-called normal world, in the Hebrew novel, *The Chocolate Deal*, New York, 1968.

Thom **Gunn,** poet, born in Gravesend in 1929. After serving in the forces, he read English at Trinity College, Cambridge. In 1954 Gunn settled in America where he held a creative writing fellowship at Stanford University. He has published poetry extensively from his first collection, *Fighting Terms*, 1954, to *Collected Poems*, 1994. His high reputation as an innovative poet has not been maintained even though he continues to experiment with new and highly accomplished styles of writing.

Michael **Hamburger,** poet and translator, born in Berlin in 1924. His German–Jewish family came to Britain in 1933, the year Hitler came to power, when he was nine years old. Hamburger was educated at St Paul's School and at Oxford. He has published poetry extensively from *Flowering Cactus*, 1950, to the present day, see, *Collected Poems*, 1995. His highly regarded translations from the German have been wide ranging, and his critical work, *The Truth of Poetry*, 1969, commands widespread respect. His own poetry is closely wrought and conveys a sense of ubiquitous alienation.

Anthony **Hecht,** American poet, born 1923 in New York. Hecht has published verse extensively over the years and his carefully crafted work commands great respect. Hecht represents the Holocaust in the context of the many forms of evil throughout the ages. Amongst his publications, see *The Hard Hours*, 1967, and *The Transparent Man*, 1991.

William **Heyen,** American poet, born of German forebears, some of whom were Nazis. He is deeply preoccupied with these and writes almost exclusively of the extermination of Jews. See *The Swastika Poems*, 1977, *My Holocaust Songs*, 1980, and *The Trains*, 1981, all published in the USA.

Geoffrey **Hill,** poet, born 1932 and educated at Keble College, Oxford. His first collection of poems appeared in 1959 *For the Unfallen*, and was followed by *King Log*, 1968. Many of his poems deal with violence as well as religion. His work is powerful, oblique, ironic and deeply pondered. Its effect is often ambiguous.

Peter **Huchel,** German poet, born in Berlin in 1903, where he studied philosophy and literature. He received a prize for his first collection of poems in 1932 but withdrew his manuscript when the Nazis came to power a year later. He was an associate of Brecht and after the war his poetry was published extensively in West Germany. He died in 1981. See *Selected Poems*, 1974. In a private letter, Michael Hamburger writes of him, "he was much concerned with the Jews and wrote a prose piece about the Jewish cemetery at Sulzbach, not far from his refuge in West Germany. When I stayed with him there . . . he took me to that cemetery. I wrote a [long] poem about that stay and the cemetery: 'At Stamfen'. Huchel's poem, 'Roads', is about the exodus of Germans from Eastern Germany at the end of the war."

Randall **Jarrell,** American writer born in Tennessee in 1914. He taught in various colleges and published poetry extensively. See *The Complete Poems*, 1971. He published one well-known satirical novel, *Pictures from an Institution*, 1954, and a number of critical works and translations. He died in 1965.

Abba **Kovner,** Hebrew poet, born 1918 in Russia, educated in Vilna. During the war he was involved in armed resistance in the

Vilna Ghetto, escaping to lead Jewish partisan units in the neighbouring forests. From there he made his way to Cairo where he was imprisoned by the British for participating in Jewish-survivor rescue operations (beriha). In 1946 Kovner settled in a kibbutz in Israel. His poetic sequence, *My Little Sister*, 1967, alludes repeatedly to biblical and traditional Jewish imagery, thus distancing and lending further significance to the details of the Holocaust to which the stanzas refer throughout. See *Selected Poems* (with Nelly Sachs), 1971.

Lotte **Kramer,** poet and translator, was born in Mainz in Germany and came to England as a child refugee in 1939. Her work has appeared in a wide range of periodicals and anthologies and her poetry has been broadcast on BBC radio and television. She has published extensively, from *The Shoemaker's Wife*, 1987 to *The Desecration of Trees*, 1994. Her poetry may be compared with that of Karen Gershon.

Denise **Levertov,** born in England in 1923. Her mother was Welsh and her Russian-Jewish father became an Anglican clergyman. She married an American and settled in the US in 1948. She has published collections of verse extensively from 1946 to the present day, and her work is especially well known in America. In particular see *The Jacob's Ladder*, 1961.

Primo **Levi,** Jewish-Italian poet and writer, born in Turin in 1919. Before the war he was an industrial chemist, but in 1943 was arrested and deported to Auschwitz. His most famous prose work, *If This is a Man*, published in England in 1960, is about his experiences in Auschwitz which he survived on account of his usefulness as a chemist to the Nazis. Other important accounts followed. His poems are gathered together, in translation, in the *Collected Poems*, 1988, translated by Ruth Feldman and Brian Swann. Primo Levi continued to be haunted by his war time experience and committed suicide in 1987. (Compare Paul Celan and Tadeusz Borowski.)

George **Macbeth,** Scottish poet, novelist and broadcaster, born in Lanarkshire in 1932. He produced arts programmes for the BBC between 1955 and 1976. In the 1960s he was associated with the fashion for performance poetry. His early poetry was experimental and he later continued to use violent or macabre images. He wrote

213

a number of poems on or using Holocaust imagery. See *The Colour of Blood*, 1967, and *Poems of Love and Death*, 1980. He died in 1992.

Czeslaw **Milosz,** Polish poet, born in Lithuania in 1911. He studied law at the University of Vilnius and first published poetry in 1933. He was a member of the Polish Underground during the war, editing anti-Nazi poetry. After the war he served as a Polish cultural attaché in Paris and Washington. In 1960 he became Professor of Slavic Literature at the University of California in Berkeley. He has published poetry and prose extensively and has translated in both directions. He was awarded the Nobel Prize for Literature in 1980. See *Collected Poems*, 1988.

Martin **Niemöller,** German pastor and theologian, born Lippstadt, Germany 1892. When Hitler came to power he first went along with him as he was an anti-Communist, but became disillusioned when Hitler insisted on the supremacy of the state over religion. Niemöller became the leader of a group of German clergymen who were against Hitler but, unlike himself, they capitulated under the threat of Nazi persecution. Hitler detested Niemöller personally and had him arrested and eventually confined in the concentration camps of Sachsenhausen and Dachau. Niemöller was released in 1945 by the Allies and continued his career in Germany as a clergyman and as a noted pacifist. See *Here Stand I*, 1937, USA.

Dan **Pagis,** a Hebrew writer, born in 1930 in Bukovina of German-speaking parents. He spent some of his early years in a concentration camp in the Ukraine, from which he escaped before the end of the war. He then settled in Israel where he eventually taught medieval Hebrew literature at the University of Jerusalem. Though originally German-speaking, he deliberately cultivated modern Hebrew as his only poetic language. His references to the Holocaust are sometimes oblique and filtered through his use of biblical images and imaginary conversations with a ghost of himself who has erroneously survived. His poetry has been widely translated. See his *Selected Poems*, 1976.

János **Pilinszky,** Hungarian poet and dramatist, born in Budapest in 1921. During the war he spent some time in the camps. Afterwards he published poetry extensively in Hungarian, continuing to identify with Holocaust victims throughout his writing career. He died in 1981. His intense, concentrated, pared-down style has been compared with that of Samuel Beckett. He regarded the suffering in the death camps as a spiritual paradigm of the modern world. His work is translated and introduced by Ted Hughes in *Selected Poems*, 1976.

Sylvia **Plath,** American poet and novelist, born in Massachusetts 1932. She was famous for her nervous breakdowns which fuelled her work. She married the poet Ted Hughes and came to live in England, where she finally committed suicide in 1963. She published a number of collections of poetry from *The Collosus*, 1962, to her posthumous *Collected Poems*, 1981, which was awarded the Pulitzer Prize. Her imagery is always powerful and uses Holocaust terms in an everyday way to reinforce her meaning.

Vasko **Popa,** Serbo-Croat poet and editor, born 1922 in northern Yugoslavia. He has published collections of poems since 1952 and his work has been widely translated. He witnessed Nazi atrocities in Serbia during the war, as well as the barbarities of the pro-Nazi Croatian death squads. Popa's admirable translations into English are by Anne Pennington (now deceased). His language is spare and objective, his poetic constructions cyclical. He is a difficult poet to whose use of myth Ted Hughes is drawn. See Popa's *Collected Poems 1943–76*, published in 1976.

Peter **Porter** is a fifth-generation Australian on his father's side. He came to England in 1951 where he has lived ever since, though he makes yearly forays to Australia. Peter Porter is a well-known poet, literary journalist and radio broadcaster. He is married and has two grown-up daughters. He has written poetry extensively. 'Annotations of Auschwitz' was written in 1960 for the composer David Lumsdaine to set as a cantata. 'May, 1945' was written in 1970 in response, the poet writes, 'to long-held feelings about Germany's Jekyll-and-Hyde psychic personality'. See *Collected Poems*, 1984.

Miklós **Radnóti,** Hungarian poet of Jewish descent, born Budapest 1909. Author of six volumes of poetry including *Steep Road*, 1938, for which he was awarded a prestigious prize. His work showed his indebtedness to the classical poets as well as to French poets of the early 20th century. During the war Radnóti was imprisoned in a concentration camp in Bor, Yugoslavia. His body was found in 1944 in a mass grave, a roll of his manuscript poems stuffed into his coat pocket. See *Clouded Sky*, 1972, USA and *Subway Stops*, translated by George Emery, 1977, Ann Arbor, USA.

Anne **Ranasinghe,** poet, born as Anneliese Katz in Essen, Germany. She was brought to England in 1939, the only one of her family to be rescued from the Nazis. She trained as a journalist and married a university professor from Sri Lanka where she now lives. She began to write in 1969 and her poems have appeared in a number of periodicals and have been anthologized world-wide. A collection of her poems, *You Ask Me Why I Write*, appeared in Germany in 1994. Her work may be compared with that of Lotte Kramer and Karen Gershon.

Charles **Reznikoff,** Jewish-American narrative poet, 1894–1976, who has published extensively. He was educated as a lawyer and then went into journalism. Both of these disciplines trained him to present facts with straightforward immediacy without commenting on them directly. The contents of his long poem *Holocaust*, 1975, was based on details taken from the Nurenberg and Eichmann trials.

Tadeusz **Różewicz,** Polish poet, was born in Radomsko, central Poland. He was involved in the Polish Resistance and after the war studied art history at the University of Cracow. In addition to his poetry, Różewicz has written prose and drama. His work has been translated into many languages and in 1966 he was awarded Poland's most prestigious literary award, the State Prize for Literature, First Class. As a witness of the German Occupation in Poland, Różewicz wrote, 'What I produced is poetry for the horror-stricken. For those abandoned to butchery. For survivors.' His poetics is pivotal to our understanding of post-war aesthetics (see Introduction). Adam Czerniawski's admirable translations of his poems are to be found in *They Came to See a Poet*, 1991.

Nelly **Sachs,** poet, born in Berlin in 1891. Being Jewish she emigrated to Sweden in 1940. She supported herself as a translator. She first published poetry in Germany in 1921, then more extensively after the war. Her poetry draws on biblical models, in particular the tradition of Lamentations. Though geographically distant from the death camps themselves, she nevertheless participated imaginatively in the destruction of her people and sought to speak for those who could not speak for themselves. She was awarded the Nobel Prize for Literature, together with S. Y. Agnon, in 1966. She died in 1970. See *Collected Poems*, 1968, and *Selected Poems* (with Abba Kovner), 1971.

Hilda **Schiff,** poet, short story writer and editor, was born in central Europe and came to England as a small child. She was educated at the Universities of London and Oxford, in both of which she formerly taught and engaged in research. She is attached to Wolfson College, Oxford, and is now a freelance writer. Her publications include a collection of poems, *A Condition of Being*, 1964, and *Contemporary Approaches to English Studies*, 1977. Her work has appeared in anthologies and periodicals, and one of her poems forms part of the RSGB's prayer book.

Anne **Sexton,** American poet, born in Newton, Massachusetts 1928. Her poetry was linked to that of Robert Lowell in being 'confessional' or concerned with the details of daily life and their significance to the self. She published extensively from 1960 onwards until she committed suicide in 1974. See her posthumously published *The Awful Rowing Towards God*, 1975, and *The Selected Poems of Anne Sexton*, 1991.

Alan **Sillitoe,** poet and novelist, born in 1928 in Nottingham. He made his fame depicting recalcitrant working class anti-heroes in novels and short stories, see *The Loneliness of the Long-Distance Runner* (1959). Much of his prose work has been made into films. He has published several volumes of poetry. See *Collected Poems*, 1993.

Antoni **Slonimski,** Jewish-Polish poet and playwright, born in Warsaw in 1895. He avoided the German Occupation of Poland by managing to get to England but returned to Poland after the war and joined a group of Polish intellectuals who were against the totalitarian ideology then prevailing. His collection of poems, *Alarm*, 1941, concerning the war, was published in Polish in London. There are no English translations of his work as a whole. He died in 1976.

Boris **Slutsky,** Russian-Jewish poet, born 1919 in the Ukraine. He served in the Soviet Army during the war and witnessed terrible scenes at the front. Amongst Russian speakers he has a very well-established literary reputation and he has published several collections of poems. His first collection, *Memory*, came out in 1957 in Russia. His collections are not available in English translation.

W. D. **Snodgrass,** American poet, born in Pennsylvania in 1926. His first collection of poems, *Heart's Needle*, 1959, with its theme of separation, won the Pulitzer Prize. Snodgrass continued to publish verse and in 1977 wrote a long series of dramatic monologues in *The Fuehrer Bunker*. In this original work the major Nazis, at the end of the war, express their own deeply perverted points of view. See *Selected Poems*, New York, 1987.

Stephen **Spender,** poet and literary critic, was born in London in 1909. While at Oxford in the early 1930s he met W. H. Auden and Christopher Isherwood and together they made a considerable impact on the literary scene. Spender stayed for a while in Berlin before the war and also went to Spain during the Civil War to show solidarity with the anti-fascist forces there. He has published poetry extensively since his first volume, *Poems*, 1933, to *Collected Poems*, 1985, and *Dolphins*, 1994. His early autobiography, *World Within World*, 1951, is a sensitive study not only of himself personally but also of what Churchill was later to call 'the gathering storm'. Spender has held a number of university posts both in America and in Britain. He was awarded a knighthood in 1983.

Abraham **Sutzkever,** Yiddish poet and editor, born 1913 in Belorussia. His family settled in Vilna in 1922, and he first published poetry in 1934. Like Abba Kovner, Sutzkever was prominent among the organizers of the Vilna Ghetto Underground, encouraging literary activities and ghetto theatre. Subsequently he participated in partisan fighting in the surrounding forests. Throughout this time he continued to write poetry copiously and managed to preserve it. His work was not published until 1979 under the title *The First Night in the Ghetto*, Tel-Aviv. See also, *Burnt Pearls: Ghetto Poems*, 1981, USA.

Anna **Swirszczynska** was born in Warsaw (1909–1984) where she obtained a University education. During the war she was involved in the literary underground. Later she became a children's writer and was known as Anna Swir. She published extensively in prose and also published nine volumes of poetry. She speaks of the horror of her own and her neighbours' experience under the Nazis with cool objectivity. Her collection of poems *Building the Barricade* (in Polish and English) appeared in 1979 in Cracow.

David **Vogel,** Jewish poet who wrote in Hebrew. Vogel was born in 1891 in Russia and grew up in Vilna and Lvov. As a young man he settled in Vienna where he was arrested as a Russian enemy alien during World War One. Afterwards he settled in Paris and with the onset of the Second World War he was arrested again, this time as an Austrian enemy alien. In 1944 he was arrested yet once more by the Nazis and thereafter disappeared, presumably deported. His lyrical verse has a dreamlike sense of foreboding and fatalism, underpinned by stoicism. See *Selected Poems*, 1976.

Elie **Wiesel,** Jewish poet, born in Hungary in 1928. During the war he was deported with his family to Auschwitz where they perished but he alone survived. Wiesel was then sent on to Buchenwald. After liberation he settled in Paris. He finally migrated to the US where he is Andrew Mellon Professor in the Humanities in the University of Boston. He is also Chairman of the President's Commission on the Holocaust. He first stunned the literary world with his book *Night*, 1958 (original English translation 1960), which depicts life and death in the camps. Since then he has published extensively and has received immense international acclaim including the Nobel Prize in 1986. Amongst other works, see the less well-known cantata text, *Ani Maamin, A Song Lost and Found Again*, New York 1973.

Itamar **Yaoz-Kest,** Hebrew poet and novelist, born in 1934 in Szarvas, Hungary. He spent 1944–45 imprisoned in Bergen-Belsen, and in 1951 settled in Israel where he studied at the Hebrew University, and since 1958 has been editor at Eked Publication House. His publications are numerous and include his first poetry collection, *Angel Without Wings*, 1959, Israel, and *Vista of Smoke*, 1961. He has also published a number of highly regarded novels.

Yevgeny **Yevtushenko,** Russian poet, born 1933. He was the most notable and most popular poet of the post-Stalin generation, drawing huge audiences to his readings. His poems expressed faith in the future, as well as the need to be honest and direct, and not to cover up the truth. Some of his poems were more controversial, such as 'Babii Yar' (a place-name for a ravine on the outskirts of Kiev where Nazi forces mass-murdered tens of thousands of Russian Jews – for years the Soviets had ignored the site of this atrocity altogether and then failed to mention that it was a mass graveyard specifically for Jews). Yevtushenko's poem implied that anti-Semitism was still active in Russia, and he eloquently identified himself with the long history of Jewish suffering in that country. This earned him widespread disapproval. See *The Collected Poems, 1952–1990*, edited by Albert C. Todd, 1991.

Natan **Zach**, Hebrew poet, born in Berlin in 1930. In 1935 his family migrated to Israel and he eventually served in the Israeli army. Zach is a translator into Hebrew of Brecht, Dürrenmatt, Frisch and Strindberg. Between 1968 and 1979 he settled in the UK but in 1979 he returned to Israel to teach in the University of Haifa. In 1981 he was the recipient of the Bialik Prize, Israel's most prestigious literary award. His translated poems appear in *Against Parting*, Newcastle, 1967, and in *The Static Element*, New York, 1982.

Adam **Zych**, Polish poet, essayist and translator, born 1945 in Czestochowa, Poland. He is Professor of Pedagogics at the University of Kielce. Zych is the recipient of many awards and the editor of several volumes of an anthology entitled *Auschwitz Was in My Land*, 1987 and 1993, published by the Auschwitz Museum. His own collections of poems are *The Bridge*, 1983 and *Departure is in Us*, 1993.

INDEX OF POETS

Index of Translators

INDEX OF TITLES

INDEX OF FIRST LINES

Acknowledgements

The editor wishes to acknowledge a variety of contributions made by the following persons in the compilation and editing of this collection: Dr Glenda Abramson, Professor Alice Eckhardt, Mr Michael Hamburger, Mrs Tanya Joyce, Professor Walter Laqueur, Dr Sybil Rosenfeld, my editor, Mr Giles Semper and his team, Professor Jon Stallworthy, Mrs Christa Wichmann, as well as all the many generous contributors to these pages and other well-wishers whose support and kind words have kept me going on darker days.

In particular, I would like to thank the Wiener library and its staff for their unfailing patience and helpfulness. The Wiener library is a unique institution which no worker in the field of Holocaust could ever think of doing without.

The acknowledgements pages constitute an extension of the copyright page.

The editor and publisher acknowledge with thanks permission from the poets and their publishers to reproduce copyright material. Where available, copyright information is listed below:

Dannie Abse and Sheil Land Associates Ltd for 'A Footnote Extended' by Dannie Abse, reprinted from *Remembrance of Crimes Past, Poems 1986–1989* (1990 Hutchinson Publications).

Anvil Press Poetry for the following:
1. 'Between the Lines' and 'Treblinka' reprinted from *Collected Poems 1941–1994* by Michael Hamburger (1995).
2. 'Be Seeing You' reprinted from *Complete Poems 1953–1987* by Vasko Popa, translated by Anne Pennington and Francis R. Jones (1995).
3. 'Leave Us', 'In the Midst of Life', 'Posthumous Rehabilitation', 'Pigtail', 'What Luck', 'The Return', 'The Survivor' and 'Massacre

of the Boys' reprinted from *They Came to See a Poet* by Tadeusz Różewicz, translated by Adam Czerniawski (1991).

Anvil Press Poetry and Ted Hughes for 'Harbach 1944', 'Passion of Ravensbrück', 'On the Wall of a KZ-Lager' and 'Fable' (detail from 'KZ-Oratorio: Dark Heaven') reprinted from *The Desert of Love* by János Pilinszky, translated by János Czokits and Ted Hughes (1988).

Anvil Press Poetry and Persea Books, New York, for 'Psalm', 'Zürich, the Stork Inn' and 'Death Fugue' reprinted from *Poems of Paul Celan*, translated by Michael Hamburger (1988), © 1972, 1980, 1988 by Michael Hamburger.

Black Sparrow Press, California for extracts from *Holocaust* by Charles Reznikoff, © 1975 by Charles Reznikoff.

Georges Borchardt Inc., New York, for the extract beginning 'Never Shall I Forget' reprinted from *Night* by Elie Wiesel, © 1958 by Les Editions de Minuit.

Keith Bosley, Jerzy Ficowski and the Menard Press for 'A Girl of Six from the Ghetto', 'In Memory of Janusz Korczak', 'Both Your Mothers', 'I Did Not Manage to Save', 'The Execution of Memory', and 'The Assumption of Miriam' reprinted from *A Reading of Ashes* by Jerzy Ficowski, translated by Keith Bosley and Krystyna Wandycz (1981 Menard Press).

Lily Brett for her poems 'My Mother's Friend', 'I Keep Forgetting', 'La Pathétique' and 'Leaving You' reprinted from *After the War* (1990 Melbourne University Press).

Faber & Faber Ltd and Farrar, Straus & Giroux, New York, for the following:
1. 'A Camp in the Prussian Forest' and 'In the Camp There Was One Alive' reprinted from *The Complete Poems of Randall Jarrell* (1971).
2. 'Innocence' reprinted from *My Sad Captains* by Thom Gunn (1961).

Faber & Faber Ltd, Garzanti Editore/Faber, Inc., Milan, Ruth Feldman and Brian Swann for 'Shemá', 'Reveille' and 'The Survivor' reprinted from *Collected Poems* by Primo Levi, translated by Ruth Feldman and Brian Swann (1988).

Faber & Faber Ltd and HarperCollins USA, New York, for 'Daddy' reprinted from *Ariel* by Sylvia Plath (1965).

Faber & Faber Ltd and Random House Inc., New York, for 'Twelve Songs 1' (here printed as 'Refugee Blues') reprinted from *Collected Poems* by W.H. Auden, edited by Edward Mendelson (1979).

Ruth Fainlight for her poem 'Archive Film Material'.

Farrer, Straus & Giroux, Inc., New York, for 'O the Chimneys' and 'Already Embraced by the Arm of Heavenly Solace' translated by Michael Roloff, 'O the Night of the Weeping Children' translated by Michael Hamburger, and 'A Dead Child Speaks' translated by Ruth and Matthew Mead, all reprinted from *Selected Poems* (With Abba Kovner) by Nelly Sachs (1971 Jonathan Cape).

Elaine Feinstein for her poem 'Annus Mirabilis 1989'.

Michael Hamburger for 'Roads' reprinted from *The Garden of Theophrastus* by Peter Huchel, translated by Michael Hamburger (1983 Carcanet).

Henry Holt and Company, Inc., New York, for 'Babii Yar' from *The Collected Poems, 1952–1990* by Yevgeny Yevtushenko, edited by Albert C. Todd with Yevgeny Yevtushenko and James Regan, © 1991 by Henry Holt and Company, Inc.

A.A. Knopf, Inc. for 'The Book of Yolek' reprinted from *The Transparent Man* (1991) and 'More Light, More Light' reprinted from *Collected Earlier Poems* (1991), both by Anthony Hecht.

Lotte Kramer for her poems 'The Shoemaker's Wife' and 'The Red Cross Telegram'.

Methuen London, an imprint of Reed Consumer Books, for 'How We See' from *Poems 1978–1985* and 'If' from *Plays Four*, both by Edward Bond.

Methuen London, an imprint of Reed Consumer Books, Routledge, New York, and the Brecht Estate for '1940', translated

231

by Sammy McLean, 'The Burning of the Books', 'I, the Survivor', 'War Has Been Given a Bad Name', translated by John Willett, reprinted from *Bertolt Brecht Poems 1913–56*, edited by John Willett and Ralph Mannheim (1976).

New Directions Publishing Corp., New York, and Lawrence Pollinger Ltd for 'During the Eichmann Trial', reprinted from *Poems 1960–1967* by Denise Levertov, © 1966 by Denise Levertov.

Oxford University Press and Peter Porter for 'May, 1945' and 'Annotations of Auschwitz' from *Collected Poems* by Peter Porter (1984).

Penguin Books Ltd for 'Heritage' by Hayim Gouri, reprinted from *The Penguin Book of Hebrew Verse*, edited by T. Garmi (1981).

Penguin Books Ltd and Ecco Press, New Jersey, for 'A Poor Christian Looks at the Ghetto' and 'Campo dei Fiori', reprinted from *The Collected Poems 1931–1987* by Czeslaw Milosz (1988 Viking), © Czeslaw Milosz Royalties Inc., 1988.

Penguin Books Ltd and Dufour Editions Inc., Pennsylvania, for 'September Song' reprinted from *King Log* (1968 Andre Deutsch) and 'Ovid in the Third Reich' reprinted from *Collected Poems* (1986 Andre Deutsch), both by Geoffrey Hill.

Peters Fraser & Dunlop Group Ltd for 'A German Requiem' reprinted from *The Memory of War and Children in Exile* by James Fenton (Penguin).

Princeton University Press, New Jersey, for 'He Was Lucky' by Anna Swirszczynska, translated by Magnus J. Krynski and Robert A. Maguire, reprinted from *Building the Barricade* (1979).

Anne Ranasinghe for her poem 'Holocaust 1944'.

Random House, Inc., New York, for the following:
1. Extracts from 'Ani Maamin, A Song Lost and Found Again', reprinted from the Cantata of the same title by Elie Wiesel (1973).
2. 'Passover: the Injections' and 'Riddle', reprinted from *The Swastika Poems* by William Heyen (1977 Vanguard Press).

Random House UK Ltd and Sterling Lord Literistic Inc., New York, for 'After Auschwitz', reprinted from *The Awful Rowing Toward God* by Anne Sexton (1977 Chatto & Windus).

Anthony Rudolf, the Menard Press and The Institute for the Translation of Hebrew Literature, Israel, for 'How Can I See You, Love', 'I Saw My Father Drowning', 'There is a Last Solitary Coach', reprinted from *Selected Poems* by David Vogel, translated by A. C. Jacobs (1976). World translation rights by The Institute for the Translation of Hebrew Literature.

Hilda Schiff for her poems 'Discovery', 'When It Happened', 'The German Frontier at Basel', © Hilda Schiff. Reproduced by kind permission of the author.

Howard Schwartz for 'Elegy' by Antoni Slonimski, translated by Isaac Komen, reprinted from *Voices Within the Ark: The Modern Jewish Poets*, edited by Howard Schwartz and Anthony Rudolf, © 1980.

Secker & Warburg, an imprint of Reed Consumer Books, for 'A Poem of Death' reprinted from *Poems of Love and Death* by George Macbeth (1980).

Alan Sillitoe for 'Synagogue in Prague' reprinted from his *Collected Poems* (1993 HarperCollins).

SCM Press and Simon & Schuster Ltd, New York, for 'Who Am I?' reprinted from *Letters and Papers from Prison* (Revised, Enlarged Edition) by Dietrich Bonhoeffer, © 1953, 1967, 1971 by SCM Press Ltd.

Soho Press, New York, for 'Magda Goebbels' from 'A Darkling Alphabet', reprinted from *Selected Poems* by W. D. Snodgrass (1987).

Sir Stephen Spender for his poems 'History and Reality' reprinted from *Dolphins* (1994, Faber & Faber) and 'Memento' reprinted from *The Terrible Rain – The War Poets*, edited by Brian Gardner (1966 Methuen).

Suhrkamp Verlag, Frankfurt, for 'Portrait of a House Detective' reprinted from *Hans Magnus Enzenberger: Selected Poems*, translated by Hans Magnus Enzenberger and Michael Hamburger (1994 Bloodaxe Books).

Val Tripp for 'Race', 'I Was Not There' and 'Experiments with God' by Karen Gershon, reprinted from her *Selected Poems* (1966 Victor Gollancz).

Howard Schwartz and Daniel J. Weissbort for 'How They Killed My Grandmother' and 'Burnt' by Boris Slutsky, translated by Daniel J. Weissbort, reprinted from *Voices Within the Ark: The Modern Jewish Poets*, edited by Howard Schwartz and Anthony Rudolf, © 1980.

Viking Penguin, a division of Penguin Books USA, Inc., for 'Without Jews' by Jacob Glatstein, translated by Cynthia Ozick, reprinted from *The Penguin Book of Modern Yiddish Verse* by Irving Howe, Ruth R. Wisse and Chone Shmeruk. © 1987 by Irving Howe, Ruth Wisse and Chone Shmeruk. Introduction and Notes © 1987 by Irving Howe.

Adam Zych and Hilda Schiff for the poem 'Auschwitz 1987', written by Adam Zych and translated by Hilda Schiff.

Every effort has been made to trace copyright owners, and the publishers apologize to anyone whose rights have inadvertently not been acknowledged. This will be corrected in any reprint.